*There was nowhere to go
but everywhere, so just keep
on rolling under the stars.*

— Jack Kerouac

33

GETAWAYS *from*
SAN FRANCISCO *that*
you MUST NOT MISS

MARISSA GUGGIANA

emons:

Foreword

When my family immigrated to the United States, they found Sonoma County and never left. Halfway through the making of this book, I gave birth to my first child. Sharing the stories, places, and tastes of my home took on a deep poignancy. My daughter is a sixth-generation Californian and thanks to this project, she has already seen redwoods, 100-year-old grapevines, robots, rivers, and an oyster farm. They all belong to her and they all belong to you.

Within these pages I've tried to share the best places and the most representative combination of destinations. But what is the best winery? The most awe-inspiring forest? The burger you can't go one more weekend without eating? The choices I've made are well vetted, but they also naturally reflect my own biases. I believe food that is passionately prepared from quality ingredients increases happiness. If I get in the car and drive aimlessly, I will inevitably end up at the ocean. Walking amongst tall trees awakens my spirit. Not to dwell on food and drink, but you should also know that I am really into tacos, coffee, and nightcaps. Allow this to be a secret key to some of the details included in each weekend.

I can think of no other urban hub in America with a more diverse range of getaways in such close proximity. The Bay Area is so richly stocked with distinct ecosystems and cultures that you could spend every weekend exploring without exhausting your curiosity. I've picked places that I love dearly, like gentle Guerneville and inspiring Big Sur, not to narrow your list but to open up your sense of possibility. Because there are places of magnificence far beyond the 33 included here. The specificity of the weekends and the ethos of cultivating an un-obvious itinerary are tools to unlock your adventurousness.

Of course my travels were more concentrated than yours are likely to be. This intense period on the road exercised a muscle in me that I will forever be grateful for – the muscle that arrests my hesitation. It is not so hard to get in your car and see something that changes your whole perspective. It doesn't have to take a lot of money, it doesn't require months of planning. Even with a newborn, I know a new version of life that recognizes the drinking in of this enchanted place as my birthright.

– Marissa Guggiana

33 GETAWAYS

San Mateo County

Santa Clara County

Sonoma County

Yolo County

1

Mother Lode • *Gold Country & Sacramento Delta*

CALIFORNIA, AS WE KNOW IT, WAS BUILT BY DREAMERS AND RISK TAKERS, those willing to go all the way to the very end of the earth in search of fantastical wealth, fame, beauty, and adventure. That reckless bravery is the lodestone of Gold Country. Follow a time-traveling trek along the story lines of California's most gutsy pioneers – some heroic and some outrageous – all wildly fascinating.

In the 1880s, unsuccessful gold miner Walter Mercer was shooting at the rock wall of his cursed land investment one day and saw what appeared to be gold shining through a crevice. Alas, it turned out to be water and mineral content – what we know as **Mercer Caves** – but the miner turned the discovery into gold nonetheless, and started charging his fellow salty wealth seekers for the privilege of viewing the impressive formations. After paying their fee, visitors would enter with a book of matches to light their way – striking a new match when each one burned out – or would hold a candle in their mouths. Many a beard caught on fire in the pitch darkness of the still caves. That tour was a primitive version of today's experience. Later, the town used the series of caves as their own city hall and community center, and hosted church parties, wedding ceremonies, and civic meetings in various chambers. Mercer continued improving the caves throughout his life, adding stairs and a lighting system, eventually leaving them to his wife.

The formations themselves are enchanting and you can view the old-fashioned world wonder in a few ways. For the first timer, the non-clinically claustrophobic, or the creaky kneed, there is a quarter-mile walk through the main artery of the caves. A few spots along the way require ducking and there is one passage that is quite tight – just enough that you can in good faith say you went spelunking.

> TIP: *The whole tour is a shutterbug's fantasy, but the lighting is quite low, so make sure, if you are bringing a non-smartphone or non-digital camera, that you have the appropriate settings and/or film for that environment.*

If you are looking for more of an Indiana Jones type of interface with the chutes and stalagmites, you can make arrangements for genuine spelunking with a guide – sliding down and climbing up in a safe but

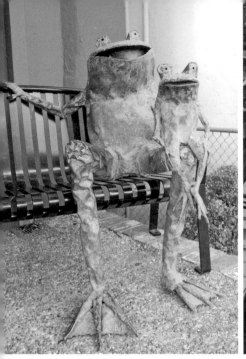

CLOCKWISE FROM TOP LEFT: *Murphys' Mark Twain frogs; Confucius at the Chinese school in Locke; Locke's entrance sign; The Shack, a gallery in Locke's historic district; Joseph Zumwalt gracing Murphys' Wall of Commemorative Ovation*

titillating tour, much like many miner 49ers surely did after their last match went out. The cave floors are slippery in many spots, so wear flat shoes with good treads to lessen the danger of an unintentional spill. The caves are just outside of Murphys, which is a prospecting town. Murphys put the rush in Gold Rush when the eponymous Murphy brothers John and Daniel became millionaires as young men and created the fantasy that had would-be prospectors frothing for years. Although a monument to Gold Country, Murphys has the charm of not being cast in amber. That is, the town maintains its old-time ambiance without being "old timey." There also happens to be a burgeoning wine industry, which gilds the town with tasting rooms and all that goes with viticulture – great food, fresh herbs, shops filled with artisanal goods.

Every Saturday at 10am you can join in a free walking tour, starting at the **Old Timers Museum** and including the home of Dr. Albert Michelson, the first American Nobel laureate, as well as a lode of Gold Rush and early Western expansion history, which flows in the heart of any Californian. Be sure to examine the western exterior of the museum for the Wall Of Comparative Ovation, a monument to local heroes, erected and maintained by the E Clampus Vitus Association (aka ECV, aka The Clampers). The wall commemorates all manner of individuals and groups, including the Chinese in California, the American buffalo, and Joseph Zumwalt, who brought E Clampus Vitus to the miners of the Gold Rush.

Tip: *Be on the lookout for frog figures, which are dotted about Murphys as a nod to Mark Twain's "The Celebrated Jumping Frog of Calaveras County." Penned in nearby Angels Camp, the short story brought him his first flush of fame, in 1865.*

Walking through caverns and downtown can give you a mean hunger. Tame the surly grumble with a meal at the **Alchemy Market and Cafe**. The food here is wine-country dining, Sierra style – juicy bistro burgers and crab cakes as big as salad plates. Main Street is a viney path of wine-tasting rooms, and the sweetest cluster is on the east end of the road, right past where Murphys Creek intersects the thoroughfare. Beautiful old stone buildings offer cool respite and the tasting culture is lively and friendly. Check out **Lavender Ridge Vineyard Tasting**, which has both excellent Rhone varietal wines and site-grown lavender and lavender goodies for sale, as well as daily wine and cheese pairings. The whole back wall of the stone barn is blanketed in bunches of the dried herb and smells just like the South of France.

End your evening at **Murphys Historic Hotel**, a former stagecoach stop built in 1856, with a New Orleansean balcony. You can stay in either a historic room, each named after one of the hotel's most distinguished Gold Rush-era guests such as Mark Twain and President Ulysses S. Grant, or a modern suite with a contemporary feel.

Tip: *Rio Vista and, more specifically, **Foster's Bighorn**, is a worthwhile detour on your way back home. The bar and restaurant are pretty down-to-earth, with one exception – the collection of 300 hunting trophies taxidermied and mounted on the walls. A relic of the 1930s and '40s romance with the safari, the place serves as a sort of stock-still zoo. And they make pretty good pie.*

An indirect route back toward San Francisco charts new territory, turning north to **Locke** and bringing you into delta country. Unless you're a sport fisherman, you may have passed by the Sacramento–San Joaquin River Delta without ever stopping or picking up its deep legacy in California history. Locke, now a part of Walnut Grove, sits a block back from the Sacramento River and is an enthralling hodgepodge of historical landmark, living town, and visitor center. People do live there now (about 80 of them) and many of the buildings house shops or museums, with apartments on their top floors. Locke (or Lockeport, as it was originally called) was founded in the early 20th century by Chinese Americans, specifically a committee of merchants, as a place for their community to design, build on, and inhabit the land of George

Locke. There is a schoolhouse, theater, gambling house, pocket park, and of course the levee. There is a riverside ramshackle vibe that makes the place a discovery for all who come, but there is also a beautiful narrative of solidarity and independence for Chinese agricultural workers and their families. Today, only about ten of the residents are of Chinese ancestry, but the historical significance is charmingly displayed and commemorated.

The path home from Locke is the last discovery on this western wander. Though you may not think of it as such, much of the land here is actually considered a series of islands, being that areas of it are surrounded on all sides by levees. Grand Island is among the biggest of these patches. It is bejeweled by **Grand Island Mansion**, the largest private estate in Northern California, built in 1917 for wealthy San Franciscan merchant Louis Meyers. Though the mansion is open only for private events, it is worth a drive-by, strangely decadent apparition that it is. Passing through the levees on two-lane farm roads before you hit the major highways, you get a final chance to take in what it must have been like, for the harebrained and heroic seekers of the past, to stumble upon this golden state.

Sacramento River, popular with fishermen, wending past Locke at sunset.

Distance from San Francisco to Murphys: *140 miles*
Drive time: *2 hours, 30 minutes*
Getting there: *I-80 E to I-580 E to I-205 E to I-5 N to CA-120 E to CA-4 E/S*

1. MURPHYS HISTORIC HOTEL: 457 Main Street, Murphys, CA
   95247, +1 800.532.7684, www.murphyshotel.com
   Details: *29 modern and historic rooms; $95–$215 per night.*

2. MERCER CAVES: 665 Sheep Ranch Road, Murphys, CA 95247
   +1 209.728.2101, www.mercercaverns.com

3. MURPHYS OLD TIMERS MUSEUM: 470 Main Street, Murphys, CA
   95247, +1 209.728.1160, www.murphysoldtimersmuseum.com

4. ALCHEMY MARKET AND CAFE: 191 Main Street, Murphys, CA
   95247 +1 209.728.0700, www.alchemymarket.com

5. LAVENDER RIDGE VINEYARD TASTING ROOM: 425 A Main Street,
   Murphys, CA 95247, +1 209.728.2441,
   www.lavenderridgevineyard.com

6. FOSTER'S BIGHORN: 143 Main Street, Rio Vista, CA 94571,
   +1 707.374.2511, www.fostersbighorn.com

7. LOCKE: River Road, about .5 mile north of Walnut Grove, CA
   95690, www.locketown.com

8. GRAND ISLAND MANSION: 13415 Grand Island Road, Walnut
   Grove, CA 95690, +1 916.775.1705, www.grandislandmansion.com

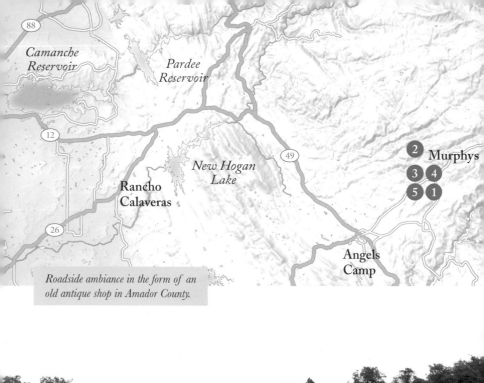

Camanche
Reservoir

Pardee
Reservoir

New Hogan
Lake

Rancho
Calaveras

Murphys

Angels
Camp

Roadside ambiance in the form of an
old antique shop in Amador County.

The Still Shining Light · *East Brother Island*

AT THE VERY POINT WHERE THE SAN FRANCISCO BAY BECOMES THE San Pablo Bay sits **East Brother Light Station,** a rocky acre of an island near the tip of Point San Pablo. Next to it is West Brother Island, where there are only birds and sometimes goats. East Brother Island remains a delicate and isolated world that has existed since the lighthouse was erected in 1874. In early days, two lighthouse keepers would cohabit the island, trading shifts. Their children would be homeschooled by a visiting teacher and supplies were gathered on occasional rowboat trips to the North Bay.

If you cross the Richmond Bridge, you may have noticed it, white and gleaming, in the distance. The island is scarcely bigger than the lighthouse and the fog signal room and it stands out among the other small islands, which are structure-less. One of the closest getaways, this is also one of the most obscure, hidden in plain sight. Ask native Bay Areans and few will have heard of this remarkable remnant of the bay's history.

Getting to East Brother Lighthouse is as esoteric as you might imagine, though not difficult. You must make a reservation so that the lighthouse keepers know to pick you up, in what is called a ferry on the website, but which is really a small speedboat, though since it does the job of ferrying, it is, strictly, a ferry. To get to the ferry from San Francisco take the Golden Gate Bridge north and then jog over tô the Richmond Bridge. You take the very first exit off the 580 after the Richmond Bridge and follow Stenmark Drive North, as it hugs the point, all the way to the **Point San Pablo Yacht Club.** You may think you are going the wrong way or going no way at all, but keep on until you end up at the marina. This is its own strange discovery, a little world of boat-centric living.

The first decision to be made is your lighthouse itinerary. You can either stay overnight or have a day visit. For history buffs and adventurers or perhaps those toting a little one, the day trip gives you ample time to absorb the story, the ambiance, and the nooks and crannies of the island, without all the downtime. Day use is only offered on Saturdays, during the summer months. You are picked up at 11:15am, when the previous day's overnight guests are taken back to the marina. After a ten-minute ferry ride, you arrive at the island, where the boat snugs up

to the perimeter and is lifted up by a system of pulleys. After you make your way onto dry land, the lighthouse keeper gives you a thorough tour of the main buildings, complete with anecdotes of lighthouse keepers past (about three dozen in all, with tenures ranging from 2 to 19 years) and the natural world surrounding and inhabiting the island, including geese nests and seals playing in the water. "Would you like to sound the fog signal?" A redundant question, the answer to which is a melancholy bellow that echoes out to sea, filling you with the humble sense of power that a lighthouse keeper must have felt on East Brother Island in its heyday. The signal would sound when the fog was too thick for approaching vessels to see the reflection from the lighthouse, originally lit with a fourth-order Fresnel lens (and later a fifth order), a stunning geometry of glass still available for viewing but no longer in use. Climb the tight, steep stairs and come up through the hatch to the widow's walk, which wraps around the lighthouse's business end and is the tallest point on the island. The walk gives you a panoramic view, brings you nose-to-beak with gulls, and dresses you in wind.

If you are a group of 6 to 12, you can arrange to have some food prepared by the lighthouse keeper and his staff (aka his wife) for your day trip. Otherwise, the kitchen is closed during island hops. But fear

not, because just before you cross the Richmond Bridge en route to the ferry is **Marin Country Mart**, a decadent mall offering many picnic-ready food options. The island has an outdoor table overlooking the water (well, what isn't overlooking the water on this island?) and indoor space if the weather is too extreme. At Marin Country Mart's El Huarache Loco, you can pick up *tostaditos de tinga* (piles of tender chicken, slow-cooked in tomatoes and chipotles atop corn tortillas) or other street-food inspired snacks. Rustic Bakery is a regional favorite for all things bready, including a crusty loaf to smother with jam and share or a perfect croissant. You can also head to Belcampo Meat Co. for beverages and sustainably raised sandwich fixings, made in-house, like their truly excellent meatballs or charcuterie. For dessert, Miette will box up a medley of macarons or lavender shortbread cookies. Once your picnic is set, it is a ten-minute drive back to the marina. After a tour, a meal, some horseshoes, and even a nap reclining on one of the sun-warmed chairs about the island, with the lulling soundtrack of water lapping, the ferry will take you back to the marina at 3:30pm.

If you would like to stay overnight, which we highly recommend, you will board the ferry as the daytrippers disembark and make that quick trip to the island to be greeted not only by the tour, but by a reception of

West & East Brother Islands, as seen from the west, in the San Francisco Bay.

CLOCKWISE FROM TOP LEFT: *Playground at Marin Country Mart; Miette macarons and Rustic Bakery coffee; EBLS ferry station on Point San Pablo; Fresnel lens in the Fog Signal Building; island in bloom; a guest room in the inn* OPPOSITE: *The Fog Signal Building*

sparkling wine and snacks. The comfortable bedrooms are all within the restrained, functional Victorian feel of the architecture. Four rooms are in the main house, where you will be served dinner and breakfast in the dining room. A fifth room is in the Fog Signal Building, which is the most secluded and has a back door that opens out to a view of Richmond and the water that feels like a secret. Dinner is a coursed event, with the husband-and-wife co-lighthouse keepers preparing lovely dishes such as chicken braised in white wine, served with asparagus and tomato bisque. A salad precedes and a dessert follows it all.

> TIP: *Because the island's water supply comes only from a cistern that collects rainwater (and is then filtered), guests staying less than two nights are asked to refrain from showering.*

If you like the B & B feel, this is a marvelous way to connect with other adventurous locals and travelers alike, sharing meals and rubbing elbows in the game room, at the horseshoe pit, or anywhere, really, on the dinky island. But outside of these gathering times, your stay is really about forced quiet. There are no televisions and the only entertainment lies in the parlor, which is filled with board games and books, many of which are lighthouse-themed. This is a spot for couple bonding, novel finishing, and meditative gazing. It is also a place to experientially absorb a whole different way of life in a whole different era. Something about the isolation and the distance from shore, not too far but far enough, allows you to squint your eyes and feel yourself there, polishing the glass along the widow's walk and guiding ships safely home.

First day of the sailing season regatta,
as viewed from East Brother Island.

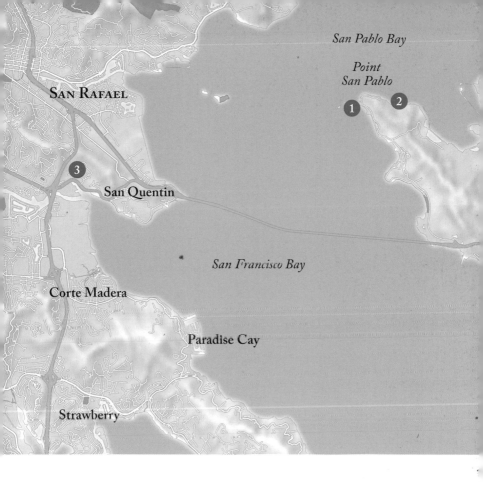

Distance from San Francisco to Point San Pablo: *28 miles*
Drive time: *45 minutes*
Getting there: *US-101 N to I 580 E to Stenmark Dr*

1. EAST BROTHER LIGHT STATION: Located on East Brother Island
   in the strait that separates San Francisco Bay and San Pablo Bay,
   CA, +1 510.233.2385, www.ebls.org
   Details: *$295–$415 per room, per night. Day use is $25 per person.
   Prices rise steeply for overnight stays around major holidays. Be prepared
   for prompt once-a-day arrivals and departures.*

2. POINT SAN PABLO YACHT HARBOR (FERRY PICK-UP AND DROP-OFF):
   1900 Stenmark Drive, Richmond, CA 94801, www.pspyh.com

3. MARIN COUNTRY MART: 2257 Larkspur Landing Circle, Larkspur,
   CA 94939, www.marincountrymart.com

What are you waiting for?

Giddy Kiddies • *Orinda, Lafayette & Walnut Creek*

THIS GETAWAY IS SO ACCESSIBLE THAT YOU CAN PRACTICALLY BART the whole trip. Regardless, it is full of crevices and crannies of the East Bay that you have likely never noticed, and offers a way to teach your children something important and to remind yourself of it, too: the spectacular is often right where you are and it is always possible to go to a place of quiet and walk among trees and tall grass and be in awe.

Tilden Regional Park is one of the great resources of Bay Area life, 2000 acres of wild land that you can take the bus to. It operates as a sort of nature primer for children. Begin your adventure gently, with a ride on the merry-go-round – a perfect carousel with a zoo of possible mounts, jingly music, and the smell of popcorn wafting through the air. The clicks of phone-cameras and echoes of "one more time!" ring through its arcade. Just adjacent is a petting zoo nestled in the woodsy ambiance of the park. Old MacDonald's Farm comes to life with ducks frolicking in water and goats on hind legs, awaiting contact with the next snack-dispensing young person. The animals are all in enclosed spaces and unlikely to intimidate even the smallest or most skittish of petters.

The next Tilden-for-children stop is Redwood Valley Roadway, a system of live steam locomotives scaled to pint-sized proportions. The rides are just a few dollars and begin to move you into the natural world, carrying you through the giant redwoods, where you'll feel the caress of the foggy air amid all the revved-up kid energy. Children line up on tiptoes, awaiting the arrival of the trains at the station.

You may need to come down off the mountain now. Cruise along the peaks of Tilden and drop into Lafayette, driving the scenic route, ignoring highways, just this once. Superimposed on this place of gentle beauty, Lafayette is a town made for families. **The Cooperage American Grille,** the enclave's most popular restaurant, belongs to a local family, the McCormicks – the same McCormicks who own the McCormick & Schmicks steakhouse chain. The Cooperage is warm and open and has something for everyone (Brown Derby salads, burgers, fettuccine) without pandering.

Refueled and renewed, head a few blocks down Lafayette's main thoroughfare, Mt. Diablo Boulevard, to **Jennifer Perlmutter Gallery**. Kid friendly and dog friendly, Jennifer has her own studio in the back of the intimate space and shows her work and others' in the front. The

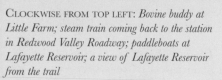

CLOCKWISE FROM TOP LEFT: *Bovine buddy at Little Farm; steam train coming back to the station in Redwood Valley Roadway; paddleboats at Lafayette Reservoir; a view of Lafayette Reservoir from the trail*

abstract artist will take kids into her workshop and show them how inspiration becomes art. She will even set them up with a space to make their own mini masterpiece.

Just a mile from the gallery is the **Lafayette Reservoir**. On the weekends, it is a genteel scene, filled with joggers, cyclists, and dog walkers waving hello. There is a serene pleasure to traversing the 2.7-mile exterior loop with a paved path smooth enough for a stroller. If you start the path heading west, you will quickly find the boat dock, where you can launch your own vessel or rent a paddleboat. Start the path heading east and you will just as swiftly come upon the fairy tale-themed playground, with lots of opportunities to climb, hide, and slide.

After your reservoir revelry, check in to your room at the **Lafayette Park Hotel & Spa**. A bit of luxury is called for after a long kid-tastic day, and a heated pool sweetens the deal. The hotel's location right in the center of Lafayette means you can park your car and forget about it for the afternoon in town. And they even have a shuttle service within a three-mile radius of the hotel.

TIP: *If you'd like an upscale restaurant option for dinner, Table 24 in nearby Orinda is hip but family friendly.*

If the kids are older and less sleepy and squirrelly in the evenings, **California Shakespeare Theater**, or Cal Shakes as it's called, is a memorable experience. An artistic institution located in the hills just east of the Caldecott Tunnel, its season runs May through October, months warm enough to take advantage of the outdoor seating, and the roster includes lively versions of Shakespeare, with some modern classics thrown in.

Sunday morning is rush hour at **Chow** in Lafayette. A regional restaurant chain, this location has long been a place to see and be seen, and is absolutely welcoming to all ages, especially during the clang of the brunch hour. Sit down and order or head to their grocery and to-go section and pick up a pastry and coffee for your deeper dive into Contra Costa's beauty.

Tilden awaits you again with an up-level hike. After the steam trains and the carousel, you have only brushed the surface of what is available here. The park is just crammed with great trails, depending on your appetite and goals. Tower Trail is a short but steep hike that ends in a glorious view with a perfect picnic spot (and has relatively fewer hikers because it isn't signposted) and starts on Grizzly Peak Boulevard, just north of South Park Road. A level and gentler hike with open vistas and a parking lot (and therefore more people) begins at Inspiration Point. Spend the late-morning hours viewing the scope of the entire Bay Area. Play "How many bridges can you spy?" with your apprentice hikers.

The last diversion in this crammed-full-of-young'un-fun, deep East Bay weekend is the **Lindsay Wildlife Experience,** a fantastic wormhole into the worlds of beasts great and small. The center is a museum and refuge center for the animal kingdom. Their weekend schedule is packed with activities like watching owls eat, petting raptors, going behind the scenes at the pet hospital, and learning the difference between wild and domestic animals (and playing with them, too). Lindsay teaches empathy and engagement with the natural world and is geared toward a child's perception.

Take the drive home, enjoying the napped-out silence in the backseat and the deep satisfaction that you have shared a sliver of the Earth's great beauty with your children.

Distance from San Francisco to Lafayette: *22 miles*
Drive time: *30 minutes*
Getting there: *80 E to CA-24 to Oak Hill Rd*

1. LAFAYETTE PARK HOTEL & SPA: 3287 Mt. Diablo Boulevard, Lafayette, CA 94549, +1 925.263.1725, www.lafayetteparkhotel.com
Details: *$189–$350 per night. On-site spa and restaurants.*

2. TILDEN PARK: 2501 Grizzly Peak Boulevard, Orinda, CA 94563, www.ebparks.org/parks/tilden

3. THE COOPERAGE AMERICAN GRILLE : 32 Lafayette Circle, Lafayette, CA 94549, +1 925.298.5915, www.thecooperagelafayette.com

4. JENNIFER PERLMUTTER GALLERY: 3620 Mt. Diablo Boulevard, Lafayette, CA 94549, +1 925.284.1485, www.jenniferperlmuttergallery.com

5. LAFAYETTE RESERVOIR: 3849 Mt. Diablo Boulevard, Lafayette, CA 94549, +1 925.284.9669, www.ebmud.com/recreation/east-bay/lafayette-reservoir

6. TABLE 24: 2 Orinda Theatre Square #153, Orinda, CA 94563, +1 925.254.0124, www.table24orinda.com

7. CAL SHAKES: 100 California Shakespeare Theater Way, Orinda, CA 94563, +1 510.548.9666, www.calshakes.org

8. CHOW: 53 Lafayette Circle, Lafayette, CA 94549, +1 925.962.2469, www.chowfoodbar.com

9. TOWER TRAILHEAD, TILDEN PARK: Grizzly Peak Boulevard, Orinda, CA 94563, www.ebparks.org/parks/tilden

10. INSPIRATION POINT, TILDEN PARK: Wildcat Canyon Road, Orinda, CA 94563, www.ebparks.org/parks/tilden

11. THE LINDSAY WILDLIFE EXPERIENCE: 1931 First Avenue, Walnut Creek, CA 94597, +1 925.935.1978, www.lindsaywildlife.org

Mountaintop vista of lush Contra Costa County in Tilden Regional Park.

Briones
Regional
Park

11

680

Walnut
Creek

10

2

Tilden
Regional
Park

Orinda

24

24

1

Lafayette

9

5 4 3

8

BERKELEY

7

6

Lafayette
Reservoir
Recreation
Area

680

Victorian Haunts • *Port Costa & Benicia*

AT THE END OF THE 19TH CENTURY, LITTLE TOWNS ALONG THE Carquinez Strait, a northern extension of the San Francisco Bay, were bustling with industry. Over the years, the strait was silted in and the railroad found more direct routes. As a result, these hamlets lost their economic importance and, eventually, their populations. Some of the towns are only memories, such as Eckley, which was a significant brick-producing center. Now its name remains only on a fishing pier, which is surrounded by a brick-strewn beach and detritus from the former factory. A few of these villages have grown and become suburban communities. And one has remained as a ghostly and quirky unincorporated town that will instantly induct you into the sacred order of "Those Who Have Discovered Port Costa."

Port Costa is so close to San Francisco that it is absurd how distant it feels and how few people know about it. But once you get off Highway 80, at Crockett, you will understand why it remains a well-kept secret. The road to Port Costa is an oak-strewn, windy meander along the strait. Just as you feel that you can't possibly be headed anywhere except to the middle of a grazing pasture, you drop onto the town's main street (and one of its only streets), Canyon Lake Drive. The road dead-ends at the municipal parking lot, as rocky and potholed as the surface of the moon (and your first taste of the wabi sabi on which you are about to feast).

This Victorian ghost town is also a notorious biker hangout. Yes, many cyclists end up here, as the roads are perfect for a challenging and picturesque ride, but we are talking about the "other" bikers. The **Warehouse Café**, a bar/restaurant that shares a building with the post office, is the center of activity for these longtime devotees, and they have kept the town on the map through many decades of change.

> TIP: *Sundays are the busiest days in Port Costa (in fact, most of the businesses are only open on the weekends). Summer Sundays are big motorcycle gathering days. To see the full splendor, plan to come then. If you prefer a little more quiet, focus your getaway on a Saturday.*

During the summer, the Warehouse will often have live bands on their "patio," which has the vibe of an abandoned carnival. And if you are too

hot in the East Bay sun, you can wander inside, where you will be delighted by a Mad Maxian assortment of Americana: a taxidermied polar bear in full rear, posters of yesteryear, an Elvis lamp. It resembles a sort of tree house for grown-ups. Don't worry if you don't own a Harley and leathers, all are warmly welcomed. At the very back of the bar is a little shop filled with vintage clothes, girlie magazines, candy, lingerie, and cowboy hats.

Stay at the **Burlington Hotel** in Port Costa and spend a weekend absorbing this rich slurry of hidden Bay Area cultures. The hotel itself is an offbeat mix of old and new. The rooms are named after former ladies of the evening and have a fixed-up, broken-down glamour. Ask for a room with its own bathroom, or take a less expensive option with a shared bath. In the morning, have your breakfast in the Honey House Café downstairs and enjoy your complimentary pour-over coffee and slice of owner Earl's corn bread, a recipe from his Louisiana family tree.

TIP: *In early July, a massive blackberry bush along the train tracks is heavy with fruit. Take your coffee and corn bread, pick handfuls of berries, and sit on the thin slip of beach.*

Amongst the quirkiness is **Theatre of Dreams**, a shop open only on Saturdays, filled with handmade, vintage-inspired ephemera, a Port Costa haberdashery, and the Compulsive Peddler, an antique shop. But the dueling pillars of the community are the town's only two eating establishments. On one side of the street is the aforementioned Warehouse, and on the other is the **Bull Valley Roadhouse**, a locally sourcing, fine-dining restaurant with a winking sense of place and fabulous pre-Prohibition cocktails. The food is served family style, which is convenient since you will most certainly be sticking your fork into everything. Dinner at the Roadhouse and a nightcap at the Warehouse offer the best of Port Costa.

TIP: *Stop by the bar at the Bull Valley Roadhouse in late afternoon and order a cocktail and an appetizer as a pre-dinner bite. Their chicken wings, pork ribs, and friend green beans all transcend expectations and re-define the dish.*

If you aren't busy creating or dispelling a hangover, the town of 200 is completely surrounded by stunning parkland. What keeps Port Costa delightfully contained is that it cannot grow in any direction. A hike that peaks in bay views can be started from any of the three main roads. Or you can always take your Hog.

Across the bay is Benicia, a sort of sister city (the older, more mature sister) to Port Costa. In the late 1800s, the towns had a strong commercial relationship, as the Solano ferry, the biggest ferry in the world at that time, would travel from Benicia to Port Costa, carrying commercial

CLOCKWISE FROM TOP LEFT: *The visitor center in Benicia; Victoriana goods at Theatre of Dreams; one of the Burlington Hotel's colorful guest rooms; Bull Valley Roadhouse; corn bread and biscuits at Honey House Café*

goods to be loaded onto a train heading to Oakland's port, until it was retired in 1930. Benicia also has Victorian bones, but it has filled out around them in a different way. Here you will find a place not looking to stay hidden, but opening its doors widely to the outside world.

A walk along the strait is a judicious start. Benicia has a lovely walkway and plenty of benches to stop at and soak in the atmosphere. If you prefer to commune more directly with the waters, **Benicia Kite and Paddle Sports'** friendly staff offers rentals and lessons for seafaring vessels from paragliders to kayaks.

First Street is the main commercial thoroughfare of the city and holds a good day's worth of antique browsing, wine tasting, and shopping. **Sailor Jack's** is the Beniciest of the eateries. Rumor has it that this former sea captain's home is haunted by a phantom that pops pictures off the wall. The restaurant is situated with the best view of the water. Oysters, shrimp cocktail, and other seaside quarry are all served here, not to mention a good hamburger. Request table number 503 and you can see the two defining peaks of the North Bay: Mount Diablo out of one window and Mount Tamalpais out the other.

Sailor Jack's serves up classic seaside dining on Benicia's main drag.

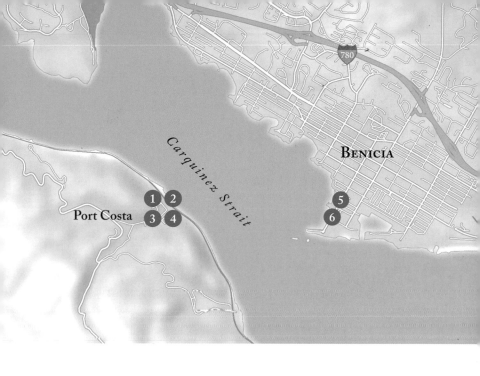

Distance from San Francisco to Port Costa: *30 miles*
Drive time: *45 minutes*
Getting there: *I-80 E to Pomona St in Crockett to Carquinez Scenic Dr to Canyon Lake Dr*

1. THE HOTEL BURLINGTON: Two Canyon Lake Drive, Port Costa, CA 94569 +1 510.787.6795, www.thehotelburlington.com
   Details: *19 rooms available and many have shared bathrooms; $85–$105 per night. Holidays book up early. No pets.*

2. WAREHOUSE CAFÉ: 5 Canyon Lake Drive, Port Costa, CA 94569, www.warehousecafeportcosta.com

3. BULL VALLEY ROADHOUSE: 14 Canyon Lake Drive, Port Costa, CA 94569, +1 510.787.1135, www.bullvalleyroadhouse.com

4. THEATRE OF DREAMS: 11 Canyon Lake Drive, Port Costa, CA 94569, +1 510.787.2164, www.wendyaddisonstudio.com, Facebook: Theatre of Dreams - Wendy Addison

5. BENICIA KITE & PADDLE: 238 First Street, Benicia, CA 94510, +1 510.900.9463, www.kiteskatepaddle.com

6. SAILOR JACK'S: 123 First Street, Benicia, CA 94510, +1 707.746.8500, www.sailor-jacks.com

What are you waiting for?

5

Clandestine Coast · *Stinson, Bolinas & Muir Beach*

IT'S NOT PRECISELY TRUE TO SAY THAT THE PLACES THAT FOLLOW ARE a secret – though the locals would prefer this to be so. But there is something romantically hidden about them. Surely you can be trusted with this information, sacred as it is. Whenever you come upon the Pacific, it feels like a discovery. In that first moment, whether you have been there a thousand times or never before, it pulls the breath out of you and takes up all your thoughts. A perfect meditation.

Among the least known, least expensive, and most gloriously situated accommodations in Marin County is the **Steep Ravine** campsite. In Mount Tamalpais State Park, perched on the coast like a hungry bird of prey, is a cluster of nine rustic cabins that don't just have a breathtaking view, they inhabit the view. The cabins themselves are simple structures built in the 1940s, with platform beds (no mattresses), wood-burning stoves, built-in tables, and large windows overlooking the ocean and a private beach. They have no running water, though there are plumbed bathrooms and a communal spigot (good for washing dishes and hands) nearby. Each comes with an outdoor barbecue, but just as with tent camping, you'll have to bring all your own gear, bedding, food, and cooking equipment. Bundles of wood, however, are available for purchase on-site.

Much like reservations for the world-famous restaurant French Laundry, bookings for any given month open up six months prior – i.e., to get a cabin anytime in August, you register online February 1 at 8am. Dylan tickets are easier to come by than a summertime reservation here. But there is total democracy to the process, because it is just luck and server speed that gets you through. Have your finger poised and information filled out at 7:59am. There are camping spots available as well, which have the same access to sky and sea and peace.

> TIP: *Sometimes it is easier to get in the day of than it is two months in advance. If you are up for a last-minute getaway, especially in cooler months, try booking for the weekend coming up and you just might be rewarded for your spontaneity.*

The entrance to Steep Ravine is a gate with a regularly reset security code (which you can request and receive a few days before your arrival

date) and once you get past that, make it down the long, steep, twisty driveway, and park your car, there is a bit of a walk. Carts are available to help you transport your things from the car. You will get to your cabin and be immediately ensconced in the quietude and dramatic scenery. Best to arrive prepared to stay all weekend, and then if you decide to venture out, so be it.

To stock up on food supplies, make a stop in the nearby town of Bolinas, three blocks of authentic coastal counterculture. This bohemian enclave is so off the beaten path, its residents are even known to take down the sign marking the turn-off from Highway One to deter visitors. Park and walk the whole town; make eye contact and smile because that's what you do here.

TIP: *If your Friday isn't complete without happy hour,* **Smiley's Schooner Saloon & Hotel** *on Bolinas's main drag is the local hangout, and as divey – and full of character – as they come. Founded in 1851, it is one of the oldest watering holes in West Marin and frequently hosts live music on weekends.*

You will not find a more delightful grocery-shopping experience than what Bolinas has to offer. **Bolinas People's Store**, tucked behind the library and set off the street, is small but well stocked. They have local breads delivered weekly, organic Straus Family dairy products, and a kaleidoscopic produce aisle. The warm-hearted staff have even created a monumental free pile, building a colorful kiosk to house the gifted goods. **Beth's Community Kitchen**, on the way out of town, makes fresh pastries for breakfast such as airy cinnamon twists and "Bo-nuts" (Bolinas donuts). Make sure you're carrying some cash in small bills because you will want to pull into **Gospel Flat's Farm Stand,** just outside of town. The robust, organic, fresh-that-day produce is available 24 hours under the honor system and has a seasonal selection, so be prepared to cook with what providence has provided. Get back to your Steep Ravine cabin by sunset, by any means necessary.

Cabins at Steep Ravine Environmental Campground offer contemplative views.

CLOCKWISE FROM TOP LEFT: *Siren Café on Stinson beach; the addictive chocolate and almond croissant from Parkside Café; the hand-carved honor-stand sign at Gospel Flats; a waterfront Bolinas home*

Saturday morning dawns on what promises to be a full day immersed in this incredible place. With your coffee in hand and your feet up on the porch rail, gaze out at the mesmerizing view and watch seals diving for fish in the surf, pelicans swooping through the salty air, and pods of dolphins wave-leaping. Time has a magical way of bending here, so don't be surprised if the lunch hour finds you still in this position. If you prefer a more active form of absorption, the hiking in Steep Ravine is spectacular, thick with redwoods and a famous ladder and wooden steps that chariot you through slippery climbs past a waterfall and creeks. **Steep Ravine Trail** dead-ends at the Dipsea Trail (part of the country's oldest footrace) and if you follow that north, Dipsea will take you all the way into Stinson Beach (12 miles, round-trip).

Tip: *With trails as varied as these, every season – every day even – will be a little different. In summer, the trails are at their most crowded, but also offer the clearest views from the ridgeline on Matt Davis, where you can see San Francisco, the Marin Headlands, and all the way to San Mateo County. In winter, the Steep Ravine section, especially, can be cold and slippery, but the landscape is at its greenest and the waterfalls and creeks are at their peak. In spring, the wildflowers are abundant; and in fall, it is clement and dry.*

By the time you arrive in Stinson, you'll be ready for lunch. Just steps from the beach, the **Parkside Cafe** offers three dining options – an old-fashioned seaside snack bar, a coffee kiosk, and a sit-down restaurant. Burgers and soft-serve from the snack bar steal the show. They also make high-quality breads and indulgent pastries, like the twice-baked almond-and-chocolate croissant. "Fair warning, they're like crack," a barista shared dryly. Indeed. There is a pocket park across the street with a little playground and plenty of shaded bench seating. The beach itself is a sandy 3.5-mile stretch with bathrooms, showers, and even a lighthouse turned restaurant, the **Siren Canteen**. It is popular for good reason.

If you are not up for such a long trek, there are plenty of nooks to explore without ever leaving the Steep Ravine campground. A short walk to the south leads to a rocky bit of shoreline that is prime for tide pooling (check the tide chart on the information board near the parking lot to find optimal viewing times). A path to the north takes you down to a pristine and secluded sandy beach where you can wade in the surf or stretch out for an afternoon siesta, hushed to sleep by the sound of the ocean breathing.

When you head out on Sunday morning, leave some time for one last commune with the coast at **Muir Beach Overlook**. Tucked back from Highway One, this vista point has a dizzying staircase leading to the edge of the cliff. If you can time your arrival to match the hour of sunset, you will take home with you the unutterable message of the cosmos, both a secret and known by all.

Produce cornucopia at Bolinas People's Store, a small grocers with a big selection.

Distance from San Francisco to Stinson Beach: *22 miles*
Drive time: *48 minutes*
Getting there: *US-101 N to CA-1 N*

1. STEEP RAVINE ENVIRONMENTAL CAMPGROUND: Highway One at Rocky Point Road, Stinson Beach, CA 94970, +1 414.388.2070, www.parks.ca.gov/?page_id=28515; online reservations: go to www.reserveamerica.com and search "Mount Tamalpais SP" Details: *9 cabins and 7 campsites; $75 for cabins and $25 for campsites.*

2. SMILEY'S SCHOONER SALOON & HOTEL: 41 Wharf Road, Bolinas, CA 94924, +1 415.868.1311, www.smileyssaloon.com

3. BOLINAS PEOPLE'S STORE: 14 Wharf Road, Bolinas, CA 94924, +1 415.868.1433, Facebook: Bolinas People's Store

4. BETH'S COMMUNITY KITCHEN: 6 Wharf Road, Bolinas, CA 94924, +1 415.868.8880, Facebook: Beth's Community Kitchen

5. GOSPEL FLAT FARM STAND: 140 Olema Road, Bolinas, CA 94924, +1 415.868.0921, www.gospelflatfarm.com

6. STEEP RAVINE TRAILHEAD : Highway One, across from the entrance to Steep Ravine Environmental Campground

7. PARKSIDE CAFE : 43 Arenal Avenue, Stinson Beach, CA 94970 +1 415.868.1272 www.parksidecafe.com

8. STINSON BEACH: 1 Calle De Sierra, Stinson Beach, CA 94970, +1 415.868.1922, www.nps.gov/goga/stbe.htm

9. THE SIREN CANTEEN: On Stinson Beach at the base of the lifeguard tower: 3201 Highway One, Stinson Beach, CA 94970, +1 415.868.1777, www.thesirencanteen.com

10. MUIR BEACH OVERLOOK: Muir Beach Overlook, Muir Beach, CA 94965, www.nps.gov/goga/planyourvisit/muirbeach.htm

Bolinas
Lagoon ①

② ③
④ ⑤
Bolinas

⑧
**Stinson
Beach** ⑦
⑨

Bolinas Bay

⑥

①

**Mill
Valley**

*Muir Woods
National Monument*

*Mt. Tamalpais
State Park*

①

⑩
Muir Beach

*Marin
Headlands*

*Steps leading down to Muir Beach Overlook's
dazzling view of the Marin coastline.*

6

Points West • *Muir Woods, Mill Valley & San Rafael*

The clearest way into the Universe is through a forest wilderness.

– John Muir

JUST ACROSS THE GOLDEN GATE BRIDGE, IN MARIN, ARE THE Muir Woods, so named after the revered American naturalist and conservationist. Sausalito and Mill Valley are so close they almost feel like a part of the city and yet they are most definitely a departure from the urbane. This weekend getaway could feel like a staycation for an intrepid San Franciscan, but once you climb to the peak of Mt. Tamalpais and look out to see a tiny skyline blinking through the fog, you will feel a million miles away.

Once the farthest point west on the scenic railroad, **West Point Inn** remains grand in its views and setting, and quaint in its modest rooms and gaslit ambiance. Before we even get to the inn, though, there are some important things to know. Unless you receive special permission due to injury or inability, the inn can only be accessed via hiking or biking. This means that you are carrying your belongings (including bedding and towels) with you, so pack accordingly. There are a few routes with varying levels of difficulty but be prepared for at least a small incline and a two-mile distance. At about the halfway mark you may think you missed a turn, until you see the inn far ahead, a hospitable beacon. The inn also has a lovely communal kitchen for you to prepare your meals, stocked with flatware, dishes, and all the usual cooking equipment, but you must bring your own fixings. There is no radio, TV, Wi-Fi access, or pay phone, and cell reception is practically nonexistent. The stay here is not about the amenities or the room, which is built to a scale of another era (aka tiny) and has one shared bathroom; it is about being perched on the ridges of Mount Tamalpais, the "Sleeping Lady," and taking your meals on the wraparound deck that dangles you above a sunset so rich it paints your memory.

TIP: *West Point Inn does book up in advance, especially on summer weekends, so be sure to plan ahead.*

When you awake on Saturday, the mountain awaits. While you breakfast, though, soak up the history lesson in the great room and

CLOCKWISE FROM TOP LEFT: *San Pablo Bay at China Camp; Quan Brothers snack shop; greenery along the trail to West Point Inn on Mt. Tamalpais; West Point Inn's wraparound porch; El Paseo's courtyard in Mill Valley; Machaca Hash at Shoreline Coffee Shop*

lobby of this longtime vacation destination. You can take advantage of the fact that you have already made it halfway up Mt. Tam and hike the rest of the way to the top. There are many gentle trails and some great mountain-biking treks. For a list of hiking trails in the park, check out www.friendsofmttam.org.

TIP: *Among the most clandestine spots on Mt. Tam is the* **Tourist Club SF** *– a hike-in-only 1915 clubhouse/German beer garden in the midst of the woods serving up lagers and snacks. Open to nonmembers only on select "guest days" and for special happenings. Check the events calendar on their website for information.*

On the off-chance you are ready to leave your mountain isolation and remix with society, spend the evening in the almost too darling town of Mill Valley, which is dusted in the feel of the mountain forest and full of excellent dining options. Have a cocktail in the atmosphere-intensive **El Paseo,** which puts the definition of cozy into another stratosphere. The Tyler Florence and Sammy Hagar-owned resto has wonderful house-made potato chips and offers a great wines by the glass list for the barfly.

The walk to your dinner reservation at **Molina** will take you through all of downtown, past the creek-draping flower shop and the boutiques and the park with the bookstore. Molina's Alan Scott oven (a famous California wood-fire oven producer) is masterfully used by chef and owner Todd Shoberg. Every dish is prepared with up-to-the-minute seasonality and accompanied by a record. Shoberg himself spins the vinyl and the playlist is printed on the menu. Dinner may be rich but you have a nice long walk to your room to work it off.

TIP: *If your weekend away lingers into the week, the* **Throckmorton Theater** *in Mill Valley hosts a somewhat legendary comedy night every Tuesday evening, sometimes featuring world-famous headliners for low ticket prices in an intimate setting.*

Sunday, pack up and head to a beachy enclave of Mill Valley for brunch in the redux diner vibe of **Shoreline Coffee Shop,** established in 1963 and serving excellent Mexicali food as well as short-order classics. Try the "Machaca Hash," a beautiful marriage of the two cultures – with hash browns, poached eggs, and sour cream – that is somehow not a gut bomb.

After breakfast, a 12-mile detour north will drop you into **China Camp,** a singular state park surrounding a small fishing village. This relatively unembellished swath of land is a historical monument and a fishing, birdwatching, and hiking destination. The park has been in danger of closure due to state budget cuts for the last several years, but it holds a unique piece of bay shoreline, protected and glassy-watered calm. The location is worth a visit just for the meditative resonance of silence there. When you arrive, take a moment to peruse the structures, including a low-key museum of an early Chinese settlement on the site. Bird lovers can while away solid hours observing the ruddy ducks, ash-throated flycatchers, and orange-crowned warblers that are drawn to the saltwater marsh and grasslands.

TIP: *On weekends, Quan Brothers snack shop in China Camp village is open and the proprietor, Frank Quan, is a local resident and shrimp fisherman.*

Taoists believe that it is impossible to be truly spiritually awake when you live in the city. And it is for this reason that San Francisco is such a wondrous place – just outside the brittle skyline is the natural world, the portal to the universe.

Distance from San Francisco to Mount Tamalpais: *21 miles*
Drive time: *1 hour*
Getting there: *US-101 N to CA-1 to Panoramic Hwy to Old Stage Rd to Old Railroad Grade*

1. WEST POINT INN: 100 Old Railroad Grade, San Anselmo, CA 94979, +1 415.388.9955, www.westpointinn.com
Details: *Seven unheated rooms with shared baths in the inn, and five cabins; $50 per person, per night for nonmembers. Two-person minimum to reserve a cabin. Pillows, blankets, and communal kitchen facility provided, but you must bring your own bed linens, food, and beverages. Select a trail to the inn from their website ahead of time, and leave your car in the appropriate parking lot.*

2. NATURE FRIENDS TOURIST CLUB SAN FRANCISCO: 30 Ridge Avenue, Mill Valley, CA 94941, +1 415.388.9987, www.touristclubsf.org

3. EL PASEO RESTAURANT: 17 Throckmorton Avenue, Mill Valley, CA 94941, +1 415.388.0741, www.elpaseomillvalley.com

4. MOLINA: 17 Madrona Street, Mill Valley, CA 94941, +1 415.383.4200, www.molinarestaurant.com

5. THROCKMORTON THEATER: 142 Throckmorton Avenue, Mill Valley, CA 94941, +1 415.383.9600, www.throckmortontheatre.org

6. SHORELINE COFFEE SHOP: 221 Shoreline Highway, Mill Valley, CA 94941, +1 415.388.9085, www.shorelinecoffeeshop.com

7. CHINA CAMP: 730 North San Pedro Road, San Rafael, CA 94901, +1 415.488.5161, www.parks.ca.gov

What are you waiting for?

Mount
Tamalpais

Corte
Madera

MILL VALLEY

Muir Woods
National
Monument

101

Tamalpais
Homestead Valley

*An island at China Camp is a popular
resting spot for many bird species.*

7

Tidal Pull • *Sausalito & Tiburon*

SAN FRANCISCO BAY IS THE INSTIGATING FORCE BEHIND MUCH OF LIFE
in Northern California. We drive above it, walk along it, ferry through
it, but how often do we engage in its waters, seek to understand its
unique impulses and history? Here is a weekend offered as a Pacific
primer, meant to whet and wet your appetite, drench it even, in the great
blue saltiness.

Sometimes the best way to understand something is to gaze at it
lovingly with a glass of bubbly. The hotel **Cavallo Point** is located
near the base of the Golden Gate Bridge on the Marin side and offers
splendid views. Spending the night is a lavish treat but even just visiting
for the day offers a sumptuous experience on the bay. The hotel is
situated in Fort Baker, a former U.S. Army post, which was clearly in
a plum spot to observe any ships seeking egress. If you do stay over,
you can choose between restored turn-of-the-20th-century rooms, once
officers' residences, and eco-chic contemporary suites. You will also have
access to their spa and fitness center, if wellness is on your weekend wish
list. There is a cooking school on the grounds in a beautifully airy space,
perfect for learning how to prepare some of the bay's natural bounty
from resident and visiting chefs. The Farley Bar, in the hotel's main
building, is the place to grab a dry martini and some warm marinated
olives and head out to the porch, where the view is at its most stirring,
especially at sunset.

On a bay-soaked weekend, traveling by sea is optimal and
approachable. **Tideline Water Taxi** offers shuttles and set itineraries,
or you can hire an on-demand water taxi and tool around on your own
timeline to locations where they are authorized to dock. Cavallo Point
happens to be one of those locations, as are all of our stops in this salty
sojourn. The taxis have beverages and snacks to make the ride even
more deluxe.

From Cavallo Point, Tiburon is a lovely next docking stop on the
way to **Angel Island**. It has a maritime feel, with its tony marina and
oceanside dining. Lunch at the old-school **Sam's Anchor Café** will give
you your seafood fix and big views of the sunny sea. Tiburon is also
home to **Sweet Things** bakery, which is perfect for grabbing a treat
(strawberry cupcake, perhaps) for the boat ride to Angel Island or for
an impromptu picnic at one of the multitudinous places on the island

where you can sit a spell, including a big lawn just a few paces past the tour bus pickup that looks out over the water and the Marin coastline. The short water-taxi ride will drop you at the commercial area of the island, where you will be given options for how to approach your day trip. There are Segways and cruiser bikes for rent and there is also an open bus tour, which follows the road running along the top of the island. There are bathrooms and a cafe, as well.

Tip: *If you aren't taking your very own vessel, Tiburon is also Angel Island's ferry landing, which you can find at 21 Main Street (www.angelislandferry.com, $15 per ticket, cash only).*

Cavallo Point, a former military compound, was transformed into a luxury resort in 2008.

There is much to this island; you can look at the aspect that interests you or soak it all up. If it is your first time, you might take the bus tour and get the lay and layers of the land. Afterward, you can hike (a total perimeter trail hike is on the easy side and takes about two to three hours, depending on your pace) or bike back to whatever may have captivated your imagination. Many come for the views, and if it's clear, the guide might describe it as a "five bridge day," meaning you can see five of the San Francisco Bay's bridges from on high (Richmond, Bay, Golden Gate, San Mateo, and Dumbarton). Before Angel Island

CLOCKWISE FROM TOP LEFT: *An old abandoned administration building on Angel Island; Tiburon ferry terminal; passionate seaman at Modern Sailing; one of Angel Island's many panoramic views; San Francisco Bay in miniature; quintessential crab roll at Fish in Sausalito*

became a state park in 1945, it was an immigration processing station and a World War II POW detention center. And before all of that, it was a home to the Coast Miwok people.

Tɪᴘ: During the winter, there is no regular weekday Angel Island Ferry service. You can, however, "piggyback" on a trip with a group that has scheduled a visit. To do this, check out the ferry's calendar on their site and arrive ten minutes before the departure time.

The 360-degree views of San Francisco Bay offer an imposing perspective of the local geography, but to really grasp the bay's reach, make a stop at the **U.S. Army Corps of Engineers Bay Model**, just 15 minutes' drive from the Tiburon ferry landing. If you are returning from Angel Island in your private Tideline, you can dock right in front of the model, which is a hydraulic replica of the bay and delta that simulates the day's tides and currents. The Bay Model is a working education center built in the 1950s to prove that a development plan to fill in the bay would be environmentally ruinous. It is free to visit, and fascinating in a no-frills way.

At the Bay Model you can dream up a sailing expedition as a prelude to a deeper dive into bay exploration at the **Modern Sailing School**, anchored in Sausalito just a seven-minute walk from the model. The expert instructors at Modern Sailing will take you on any number of preset tours or help you create your own voyage. The experience can vary from a true sailing lesson, where you will learn the literal ropes, to more of a wind-powered party, where you can grill and tan. The school can even accredit you to become a captain, if you are looking for a more in-depth education. You can also take a one-day group course, offered periodically, to learn the basics.

Tɪᴘ: If your children are the sailing students, contact the Sausalito Yacht Club for their excellent youth lessons and classes.

The salty chafe of sea air is appetite building. Six minutes on foot from the Modern Sailing School is the simply named **Fish**, which is mostly a restaurant and partly a seafood counter. Crowded? Often. Spendy? A bit. However, the crab roll is something truly special, dense with buttery crabmeat and little else. Sustainably and locally caught fish is expensive because it oftentimes costs more to do things right. There is plenty of outdoor seating but little shade, so keep your sailing cap on for lunch.

If you finish your day a bit later and want to check out the Sausalito night scene, **Bar Bocce** is right on the water. They have, naturally, a bocce court as well as a roaring fire pit with a sandy-toed roost overlooking the marina. Pizza and salads are spot-on and there is always an effervescent energy in the evenings. Navigating back to your room from your personal water taxi, your feet hardly touch the ground.

The waters between Angel Island and Tiburon are popular with sailboats and powerboats alike.

Distance from San Francisco to Sausalito: *8 miles*
Drive time: *20 minutes*
Getting there: *US-101 N to Alexander Ave to Bunker Rd to Murray Circle*

1. CAVALLO POINT: 601 Murray Circle, Fort Baker, Sausalito, CA 94965, +1 888.651.2003 or +1 415.339.4700, www.cavallopoint.com Details: *Historic or contemporary luxury lodgings starting at $300. On-site restaurant, bar, full-service spa, and cooking school.*

2. TIDELINE WATER TAXI: +1 415.339.0196, www.tidelinewatertaxi.com

3. SAM'S ANCHOR CAFÉ: 27 Main Street, Tiburon, CA 94920-2507, +1 415.435.4527, www.samscafe.com

4. SWEET THINGS BAKERY: 1 Blackfield Drive, Tiburon, CA 94920, +1 415.388.8583, www.sweetthings.com

5. ANGEL ISLAND CALIFORNIA STATE PARK: www.parks.ca.gov/angelisland

6. U.S. MARIN CORPS BAY MODEL: 2100 Bridgeway, Sausalito, CA 94965, +1 415.332.3870

7. MODERN SAILING SCHOOL: 310 Marinship Way, Sausalito, CA 94965, +1.415.331.8250, www.modernsailing.com

8. FISH: 350 Harbor Drive, Sausalito, CA 94965, +1 415.331.3474, www.331fish.com

9. BAR BOCCE: 1250 Bridgeway, Sausalito, CA 94965, +1 415.331.0555, www.barbocce.com

Gorgeous Golden Gate Bridge, from Cavallo
Point in Sausalito looking toward San Francisco.

Oyster Crawl • *Point Reyes Station & Marshall*

He was a bold man that first ate an oyster. – Jonathan Swift

INSIDE A ROUGH AND ANCIENT-LOOKING SHELL IS A CREAMY, SWEET little creature that has driven thieves to murder. Oysters elicit bold opinions. The texture and flavor tend to leave few in the lukewarm category. If you are a lover of this aphrodisiacal bivalve, this weekend will fill you with briny ardor. Lest you think oysters just an appetizer, weave yourself through the terroir, life cycle, and lifestyle of this succulence.

> TIP: *Historical perspective adds another layer of piquancy. Pre-statehood stories are well told in* The Ohlone Way, *by Malcolm Margolin, and Jack London's autobiographical* Tales of the Fish Patrol *is a fascinating look at oyster pirates from his purview as an undercover sea cop.*

If you have ever driven through Emeryville, in the East San Francisco Bay, you may have noticed Shellmound Avenue, named for the massive discard pile discovered near the shore. The Ohlone people harvested wild Olympia oysters and left the shells and other waste at sacred sites. The Emeryville mound was 60 feet high, the largest of the 400 or so other mounds found in the area. Also used as a burial ground, the site is believed to have been the repository of oyster-rich meal remnants for almost 2400 years, starting in about 800 BC. Long since covered over by construction, it was discovered in one of the first Californian archeological digs.

Olympia oysters, or *Ostrea lurida*, were a central part of Bay Area life for hundreds of years, both as a food source and as a filtration system for local waters. When the Gold Rush population boom hit, the popular protein was nearly wiped out from overharvesting. An entrepreneur named John Stillwell Morgan arrived from the East Coast and had his Eureka when he imported eastern breeds, which were larger and easier to manage than the Olympias, and raised them in the San Francisco Bay. After much experimentation, he almost single-handedly created an oyster farming industry in the late 1800s. However, soon after Morgan's death, the bay became such a bustling commercial port that pollution and heavy marine traffic once again took down the oyster population.

Now practically all of California's oysters are grown in **Tomales Bay**, which is protected as a national park.

To truly revel in a weekend of split-shelled bacchanalia, one must go directly to the source. Just north of Point Reyes Station in West Marin, the shores of Tomales Bay are only a 20-minute drive from the blustery and operatic Pacific coast, and yet a world apart. Here, the waters can be downright glassy and placid, and though the fog and wind often blow in on a whim, the surroundings remain serene.

A word of advice before embarking on this marathon: oysters are an indulgence (and a nourishing one, full of protein and iron, omega-3 fatty acids, and other minerals and vitamins). Something about them always seems to dare you to eat to absolute fullness. You must surrender to their call: you are here, in this place, and you won't be back tomorrow. The upshot is this: you are eating oysters for every meal. Of course you may balk, but the gauntlet has been thrown down.

Nick's Cove sits right on the bay and makes for a natural home base. A glamorous redux of an old wharf, the guest rooms are elegant and cozy with a nautical feel. There is an upscale restaurant where you can sample your first of many Tomales oysters to come, but perhaps the hotel's most appealing feature is the jutting pier that serves as an outpost of the bar. Just enough ambiance to embrace whatever you have in mind, romantic or raucous, the cabinette has no service, but you can bring your order with you and hole up, atop the drift of water and protected from the yank of the wind. Have your happy hour here when it is still light enough to see where you are and shake off the road.

TIP: *For a less expensive overnight option that still keeps you on the water, just across the bay you'll find the comfy and welcoming 1950s-era Motel Inverness, with room rates starting at $125 (+1 415.236.1967, www.motelinverness.com).*

When the dinner hour rolls in, drive along Highway One's meandering seascape and get to your reservation at local favorite **Osteria Stellina** in Point Reyes Station, perhaps the most sophisticated sea town in the state. Stellina is a mirror of its environment – a place that sources its ingredients from the surrounding land and water. Yes, they serve some of the best oysters around. Of course they do. They even make an excellent oyster pizza sometimes. But let's not get hung up on just that. We are dropping down into this region that oysters inhabit. Your entrée of osso buco, grass fed on the lush hillsides of Marin, is starting to tell you something about oysters, about how farmers and foragers and forests co-exist here through a spirit of collective respect.

As you're licking your plate and sipping a Nicasio-grown Pinot, you're already recognizing the dips and swerves of the route back to Nick's Cove and you're ready to appreciate the West Coast oyster all over again, come morning.

TIP: *If you get to Point Reyes Station before 6pm, stop by Cowgirl Creamery at Tomales Bay Foods and grab one of their famous local cheeses, like the triple-cream Red Hawk, to accompany you to Hog Island the following day.*

Romantic pier, ending with the bar cabin, at Nick's Cove on Tomales Bay.

CLOCKWISE FROM TOP LEFT: *Osteria Stellina's oyster pizza; bivalves with a view at the Marshall Store; Hog Island's resting tanks; the cheese case at Cowgirl Creamery; words to live by at Hog Island*

Here in West Marin, a roadside sea shanty can also be one of *Travel + Leisure*'s top 30 seafood restaurants in America. **The Marshall Store** opens at 10am and is the mandatory first stop before a day of shucking. Start easy with a plate of BBQ'd oysters from the Tomales Bay Oyster Company. Place your order and find a spot outside on the counter, which overlooks Marshall's casual-feeling marina, like a Dadaist collage of a diner meeting the ocean. As plates whiz by you while you wait – platters of big oysters bathing in chorizo butter or smoked on crostini – you may start to feel jealous, maybe your oysters Rockefeller order was a mistake. Remember that oysters magically compress to make room for more and that you are pacing yourself for a whole day. The Marshall Store has some great bottles of wine to accompany the slurping interloper – a dry, fruity rosé or maybe a toasty blanc de blanc. Add a loaf of bread and your cheeses from Cowgirl, and you are set.

As oyster farms go, **Hog Island Oyster Co.** is not the only game in town (though with the closure of Drake's Bay in 2014, they are close to the only game in town for visitors), but they just do it all so well. Drive up to the valet and feel the satisfying crush of oyster shells underfoot, walk to the check-in and cruise past tanks where oysters are sorted by size after they finish their growth cycle in the bay. This isn't a restaurant; this is an immersion. Order your oysters, get yourself set up, and elect a shucker. The time it takes the average shucker to open up a shell, loose the meat's grip from inside, and hand it off to you is the exact amount of time it takes your appetite to build for the next helping.

TIP: *To secure a table with a grill, condiments, and all the necessary shucking accoutrements (including a complimentary lesson), you'd be wise to make a reservation far in advance. This spot is jumping.*

Oysters are like the moon: they inspire poetic metaphors in even the most literal souls, precisely because they are like nothing else. But they are an expression of the place where you are sitting, looking out over the salty water and breathing in the pristine funk of low tide. Do not leave until you have absolutely had your fill. Empty your pockets and let the sun set.

An oyster orgy, as any orgy, just can't go on forever. For your morning-after, find a perfect cappuccino and pastry at **Toby's CoffeeBar** in Toby's Feed Barn in Point Reyes Station and then keep driving northwest to Inverness. Head to **Shell Beach**, a still mostly local destination that is usually not overrun. Shell Beach includes a second, pocket beach that is even less traversed and is only a bit more of a walk. There is a little parking lot at the end of Camino Del Mar Road (no signs for the beach at the main road, so stay eagle-eyed). Once you park, it is only a half-mile hike down to the shore (though, of course that means a half-mile hike back up too). Belly full and beguiled by the bay, have a swim. The waters are shallow and retain a warmth that the Pacific never hints at. You are an oyster, floating in grassy waters, content and belonging.

Retired but not forgotten, some seafaring ambiance at Nick's Cove.

What are you waiting for?

Distance from San Francisco to Marshall: *50 miles*
Drive time: *1 hour, 15 minutes*
Getting there: *US-101 N to Lucas Valley Rd to Point Reyes-Petaluma Rd to CA-1 S*

1. NICK'S COVE: 23240 Highway One, Marshall, CA 94940, +1 415.663.1033, www.nickscove.com
   Details: *Each room has an individual entrance and vibe; $225–$500 per night, depending on room, day of the week, and season.*

2. OSTERIA STELLINA: 11285 Highway One, Point Reyes Station, CA 94956, +1 415.663.9988, www.osteriastellina.com

3. COWGIRL CREAMERY AT TOMALES BAY FOODS: 80 Fourth Street, Point Reyes Station, CA 94956, +1 415.663.9335, www.cowgirlcreamery.com

4. THE MARSHALL STORE: 19225 Highway One, Marshall, CA 94940, +1 415.663.1339, www.themarshallstore.com

5. HOG ISLAND OYSTER CO.: 20215 Shoreline Highway, Marshall, CA 94940, +1 415.663.9218, www.hogislandoysters.com

6. TOBY'S COFFEEBAR: 11250 Highway One, Point Reyes Station, CA 94956, www.tobyscoffeebar.com

7. SHELL BEACH AT TOMALES BAY STATE PARK: End of Camino Del Mar Road, Inverness, CA, www.parks.ca.gov

Tomales Bay

Marshall

Tomales Bay
State Park

Tomales Bay
State Park

Point Reyes
National
Seashore

Inverness

Pt. Reyes
Station

Olema

Drakes Bay

9

A Wild Place · *Inverness & Point Reyes Station*

MARIN COUNTY IS SPECTACULAR IN ITS ABSOLUTE PERSEVERANCE TO maintain undeveloped and open spaces. The farmland trust here was the very first of its kind in the nation, and paved the way for the preservation of Marin's agricultural terrain, protecting the area from becoming the next housing-bubble darling. There is also a great deal of public parkland, and once you get beyond the Highway 101 corridor, you can feel the expansiveness of the countryside in your body. Suddenly you are a creature among creatures, inhabiting a wild place.

Inverness is one of the less touristy corners of Marin's western front and it is positioned on the Tomales Bay, though getting to your hotel will take you up into the town's wooded hills. With the feel of an expeditioner's retreat, **Manka's Inverness Lodge** may be the coziest hotel in California, filled with stone walls, wooded enclaves, leather chairs, deep tubs, and fireplaces – everywhere, fireplaces. There are a few different cabins, all luxuriantly comfortable and ranging in vibe from early 1900s hunting lodge to coastal modern.

After a fire destroyed the main lodge of Manka's in 2006 and incinerated the beloved restaurant as well, the owners opened **Sir and Star** at the Olema, just down Highway One from their property. Sir and Star is a locally sourcing fine-dining establishment with a decadence to suit any explorer's hearty appetite – short ribs, duck eggs, oysters, and bone marrow (there are plenty of green things, too!). The menu has a winking poetry to it with items such as "Faux Gras Of Local Duck's Liver, So Delicious It Should Be Illegal."

> TIP: *Stop for a nightcap on your way home from dinner at* **Vladimir's** **Czech Restaurant** *in Inverness, which has a full bar and a not-trying-too-hard 1960s bohemian vibe, in both the literal and colloquial sense of the word.*

Come morning, it is time to move from your luxury quarters deeper into the environment and shed your urban shields. First, you will need nourishment and the goodwill of the tribe. If you are in the area in summertime and early fall, these things will be found at the Saturday-morning **farmers' market in Point Reyes Station** (last weekend of June to first weekend of November). You will also find the infamous G.B.D.

(golden, brown, and delicious) grilled-cheese sandwiches, made by the crew from Osteria Stellina, Point Reyes's stellar (ahem) eatery, which compresses Marin ingredients, Italian cuisine, and attention to detail into a glorious transcendence. Made with local fixings – Brickmaiden bread, Toma from the Pt. Reyes Farmstead Cheese Co., and braised grass-fed Marin Sun beef – these sandwiches are so rich you should share them, but you can't bring yourself to do it. The prudent thing here is to eat half and put the other half in your knapsack for the hike to come. Grab some fruit from one of the farm stands and your picnic lunch is packed.

> TIP: *Both hikes in this weekend can get gusty and cold and will often take you through a few microclimates, depending on the time of year. Bring layers, a hat that won't fly away, and shoes that can stand some muddying up.*

Tomales Point Trail is an out-and-back hike, so you can always decide you have had your fill and return to civilization at any point along the

way. Making it to the very end is a challenging 9.5 miles (round-trip is 19 miles and is a long day of walking), but it will get you past almost all the other hikers and the views are an entrancement. One of the first landmarks is Windy Gap, where you will be rewarded with vistas of Tomales Bay, Bodega Bay, and the Pacific Ocean. This whole area is also the Tule Elk Preserve, a place of protection that has allowed the breed to repopulate after reaching existentially low numbers. You can see groups of up to 50 of the antlered beauties. You may also spot whale spouts in the Pacific or bobcats and coyotes jogging purposefully through the grass. Cormorants, gulls, and pelicans sail through the air.

> TIP: *When you come upon the tule elk, be respectful of their space. If they begin to retreat, you are too close. When they move out of fear, they are less likely to reproduce at the pace needed to maintain their population. In the summer, the grasses can be quite high and camouflage the elk. Be alert and steer clear of lone bucks, who can become aggressive if they feel threatened.*

Pacific views from the Tomales Point Trail ridgeline in lush February.

CLOCKWISE FROM TOP LEFT: *Tule elk herd; the Fishing Cabin at Manka's; Vladmir's, a bohemian watering hole in Inverness; wild calla lilies in Point Reyes National Seashore; sitting nook at Manka's*

Seek sustenance at sunset from Inverness's **Salt Water Oyster Depot**, a crowdsource-funded bistro with a loving gaze toward the seafood of the neighboring waters, often delivered fresh that day from fishermen just off the boat. The menu is simple and well executed, with prix fixe options and a rotating selection of oysters.

If it is a moonless night, Tomales Bay may flicker in bioluminescence, the emission of starlike lights from blooms of dinoflagellates – plankton that float near the water's surface. You can take a kayak paddle with the passionately knowledgeable staff of **Blue Waters Kayaking** and glide through this silent and magical explosion of sparkling subaquatic lights. The effect is created when the single-celled marine organisms are disturbed. Seals and night herons hunting the waters for food can set off the phosphorescence, as can schools of passing fish, which leave a shimmering trail in their wake.

TIP: *Bioluminescence tours are scheduled in advance and tend to sell out, especially toward the end of the year, when the season draws to a close, so check the Blue Waters website for dates, and plan your visit around your tour.*

Allow the call of the Point Reyes National Seashore to draw you back in for another day among the wildlife and wilderness. Start off by stocking up at **Perry's Inverness Park Grocery**, which offers hungry-hiker options to go, like breakfast burritos or their Chicken Ranch sandwich, filled with grilled chicken, sun-dried tomato tapenade, and an optional (some say mandatory) fried egg on ciabatta. Or opt for the sandwich named after the trek you are about to hit: Estero Trail, Perry's artisanal take on a BLT with avocado, herb aioli, and cheese on locally baked pullman bread.

At **Drake's Estero Trail**, you have the option of hiking the 2 mile round-trip to the bridge across Home Bay, or hiking the full 9.4 miles to Drake's Head (four hours of walking, or more depending on your pace). This is also an out-and-back trail, like Tomales Point. Starting at a defunct Christmas pine farm, which stands out from the grassy norm, you may see rabbits, mule deer, or more rarely, the white fallow deer. The full hike takes you past five estuaries, where fresh water and salt water meet at the tidal mouths of streams. Under the bridge over Home Bay, shallow water sometimes hosts bat rays and tiger sharks and at low tide, intricately patterned geometries in the mud are revealed. One of the largest populations of harbor seals in California is here, as well as some tule elk that were moved from Tomales Point.

Stretch out your drive home by returning via Sir Francis Drake Boulevard and stopping in the idyllic town of Fairfax for a bite at **123 Bolinas**. Have a milk-chocolate pudding and a glass of Meyer Family port and let the sweetness roll over you. Take home the grace of the elk, the playfulness of the seal, and the electricity of the dinoflagellates.

If the farmers market is closed, G.B.D.s can also be found on Stellina's lunch menu.

Distance from San Francisco to Inverness: *50 miles*
Drive time: *1 hour, 15 minutes*
Getting there: *US-101 N to Lucas Valley Rd to Nicasio Valley Rd to Point Reyes-Petaluma Rd to Sir Francis Drake Blvd to Argyle St*

1. MANKA'S INVERNESS LODGE: 30 Callendar Way, Inverness, CA 94937, www.mankas.com, +1 415.669.1035
Details: *$245–$815 per night. Rooms book up in advance; must call to make reservations. Beautiful breakfast included.*

2. SIR AND STAR: 10000 Sir Francis Drake Blvd, Olema, CA 94950, +1 415.663.1034, www.sirandstar.com

3. VLADIMIR'S CZECH RESTAURANT: 12785 Sir Francis Drake Blvd, Inverness, CA 94937, +1 415.669.1021

4. POINT REYES FARMERS MARKET : Toby's Feed Barn, 11250 Highway One, Point Reyes Station, CA 95956, www.pointreyesfarmersmarket.org

5. TOMALES POINT TRAIL: Trailhead is 9 miles down Pierce Point Road (after turning from Sir Francis Drake Blvd) and is marked; www.transitandtrails.org/trailheads/369

6. SALT WATER OYSTER DEPOT: 12781 Sir Francis Drake Blvd, Inverness, CA 94937, +1 415.669.1244, www.saltwateroysterdepot.com

7. BLUE WATERS KAYAKING: 60 Fourth Street, Point Reyes Station, CA 95956, +1 415.669.2600, www.bluewaterskayaking.com

8. PERRY'S INVERNESS PARK GROCERY: 12301 Sir Francis Drake Blvd, Inverness, CA 94937, +1 415.663.1491, www.perrysinvernessparkgrocery.com

9. DRAKE'S ESTERO TRAIL: Trailhead is off of Sir Francis Drake Blvd, marked "Estero Trail," www.transitandtrails.org/trailheads/368

10. 123 BOLINAS: 123 Bolinas Street, Fairfax, CA 94930, +1 415.488.5123, www.123bolinas.com

Point Reyes
National
Seashore

Tomales Bay

⑤

①

Marshall

Tomales Bay
State Park

Inverness

①

③ ⑥

⑨

⑧

⑦

Pt. Reyes
Station

④

②

Olema

Drakes Bay

Fairfax

⑩

*Misty Pacific vista along Tomales Point
Trail in Point Reyes National Seashore.*

10

Booming Boonies · *Boonville & Philo*

IS YOUR CUP A LITTLE DRY? THAT CUP THAT SHOULD RUNNETH OVER? Inland Mendocino County is the rambling trail of several winemaking appellations and ample apple orchards. Boonville, in the Anderson Valley appellation, is an agricultural oasis that has been sprinkled over with design fairy dust, giving the working town a sense of self-expression. The farming industry in this area, which has been through different iterations over the eras, is now economically grounded in the beverage business: wine, cider, and beer. And business is booming.

Traveling north draws you into the weekend in stages. Once you pass Healdsburg, 101 opens up into a country highway, two lanes of quiet freedom. Exiting onto 128, you are enveloped in the lichen-drenched landscape of Anderson Valley, first winding through the Yorkville Highland wine region and passing miles of high-altitude Merlot, Syrah, and Bordeaux varietals before arriving in Boonville.

The epicenter of the town's stylish face-lift is your lodging for the weekend: the **Boonville Hotel**, which is owned by the next generation of the family that also operates Philo's famous Apple Farm. What makes the town's vibe feel authentic is that it's an inside job. The long-thriving farming community is not being revived, it is merely adding a new layer to the richness that already hums through the valley. There are accommodations in the hotel's main lodge and satellite cabins on the property, which is festooned in sculptures, an outdoor bar, and a working garden. The decor is modern with the softly worn veneer of the country. Pillow-top beds meet chicly finished concrete bathroom floors and stacks of hipster publications like *Kinfolk* and *Selvedge*. Each room is primed to allow you a wine-country weekend – stemware and wine openers, porches that collect views, and hammocks that invite naps. That's good because this weekend can't help but get you drunk. If not on the wine, beer, and hard cider made here, then on the gentle smell of the forests, the oxbows in the Navarro River, or the electric-green hillsides of the valley perimeter.

Table 128, the hotel's on-site restaurant, is open only on weekends. Rolling into town, drop your bags and head straight into the woody-goody dining room to eat whatever is on the prix fixe menu of the night, like roti stuffed with chicken and shiitakes, wrapped in smoked Applewood bacon, and served with braised garden greens, creamy

polenta, and Basque chili cream. Return the next morning for breakfast, a simple but splendid spread – soft-boiled eggs, yogurt with granola, blood oranges, compotes, and well-made espresso drinks served in Ukiah-made mugs.

After a leisurely start to the day, saunter across the highway, which also operates as Boonville's Main Street and do a little window browsing at the Farrer Building. Two shops there, **Fish Rock Farm Girls** and the **Farmhouse Mercantile**, offer a well-curated selection of rustic goods: edible, sartorial, and collectible.

This celebratory valley has a colorful history that you can soak up at the **Anderson Valley Historical Society Museum**, a former school-house built in 1891 amid a redwood grove. One of the more compelling bits of local lore is the dying, but not dead, 19th-century jargon of Boontling – Boonville's very own language, which thrived in the relative isolation of this former logging community. You can still see it used on

bottles of Anderson Valley Brewing Company's beer, which encourage *bahl hornin'*! or "good drinking!"

Tip: *The Anderson Valley Historical Society Museum is open February through November (Saturdays and Sundays, 1pm–4pm). If your visit falls outside these months, check out the Boontling dictionary on Wikipedia, which provides enough of a selection to teach you something about the society that spoke it. A down-to-earth and vibrant lexicon, indeed.*

After this *beemsch* (attraction), you are ready for some *hornin'* (drinking), sure to be *bahl* (good). The Anderson Valley, with its chilly mornings and excellent slopes, is known for its Pinot Noirs. A luxe place to start your wine consumption is the **Madrones,** a tasting room complex, an inn, and a restaurant in the town of Philo, just a five-minute drive north of Boonville. The Spanish-style building has an olive-tree-and-stucco warmth and offers the opportunity to try a variety of different wines from the same terroir without having to travel from winery to

How green is Anderson Valley? Winter hues and vines in hibernation.

CLOCKWISE FROM TOP LEFT: *Farrer Building's country chic; Bink's tasting room at the Madrones is open mid-week; a bountiful salad at Lauren's; Philo's famous Apple Farm honor stand; Boonville beer beckons*

winery. Five or six tastes in, you'll begin to develop an understanding of what makes an Anderson Valley wine unique, what is in this dirt that manifests itself in the grapes and the glass. One thing you may repeatedly discern on your palate is apples, which are grown in great abundance around here. Layered on the terroir are stylistic choices – the rich jamminess of Bink's Pinot, as opposed to the Burgundian austerity of Knez's Pinot. **Goldeneye**, another gifted producer of Pinot and sparkling, is practically next door and there are a ton of other wonderful tasting rooms open on the weekends (but not midweek). The hotel will provide you with a map, as will almost anyone else in town, or you can just slosh down 128 from Boonville to Navarro (or Boont to Deepend, in Boontling), stopping where you hear the clink of inspiration.

Heading back to Boonville, drop by the **Apple Farm**'s honor stand in Philo. The famous fruit growers and producers of beautiful fruity confections were also the original owners of the French Laundry, before Thomas Keller bought it. The farm also has a B & B and is one of the first American farms to get into agritourism. Pick up a bottle of their hard cider or some of the same compote you enjoyed over yogurt with your breakfast at the hotel. You can find dried and fresh apples and jars of apple transcendence, in many forms.

TIP: *Anderson Valley is also the home of Bite Hard Apple Cider, which is a dry and seductive light alcoholic beverage that can be found in stores. There promises to be a cider house in the area soon, but in the meantime, check their site for locations: www.bitehard.com.*

Your Saturday dinner is where many locals will be convening, at **Lauren's**, a roadhouse with eclectic decor (think wagon wheel light fixture next to a disco ball), a stage with a piano that is often being played, and darn good food. The menu is focused on bountiful salads and Mexican-inspired dishes. The bar is pretty humming on a weekend night, but you may prefer your nightcap on that beguiling hammock dangling from your porch back at the hotel, which is, by the way, just a two-minute walk away. Sleep the sleep of the inebriated or of the just, whichever comes first.

Sunday, after breakfast, tool north to **Hendy Woods State Park**, the virgin redwood forest that will melt your mental fog with its forest-floor quietude and Navarro River gurgle. Walk until you are drunk again – this time on the quiet and freshly oxygenated air. Then head back to town and grab lunch at **Mosswood Market Café & Bakery** in the Farrer Building, known for their house-made pastries like chocolate cheese Danish or flaky empanadas with dense fillings; salads; and soups. Take your final tipple at **Anderson Valley Brewing Company**. Their daily 1:30pm tour displays their copper casks and sense of humor (their mascot is a bear with antlers: bear + deer = beer). This takes you to the end of town, the end of the weekend, but hopefully not the end of your intoxication.

What are you waiting for?

Distance from San Francisco to Boonville: *115 miles*
Drive time: *2 hours*
Getting there: *US-101 N to CA-128 W*

1. THE BOONVILLE HOTEL & TABLE 128: 14050 Anderson Valley Highway (CA-128), Boonville, CA 95415, +1 707.895.2210, www.boonvillehotel.com
   Details: *15 rooms available in the main lodge or stand-alone cabins; $140–$325 per night. Two-night minimum during peak months (May through November). Studio and Bungalow cabins are pet-friendly for a $25 fee.*

2. FISH ROCK FARM GIRLS ANTIQUES: 14111 Anderson Valley Highway, Boonville, CA 95415, +1 707.684.9739, Facebook: Fish Rock Farm Girls

3. THE FARMHOUSE MERCANTILE: 14111 Anderson Valley Highway, Boonville, CA 95415, +1 707. 895.3996, www.farmhouse128.com

4. ANDERSON VALLEY HISTORICAL SOCIETY MUSEUM: 12340 Anderson Valley Highway, Boonville, CA 95415, +1 707.895.3207, www.andersonvalleymuseum.org

5. THE MADRONES: 9000 Anderson Valley Highway, Philo, CA 95466, +1 707.895.2955, www.themadrones.com

6. GOLDENEYE: 9200 Anderson Valley Highway, Philo, CA 95466, +1 707.895.3202, www.goldeneyewinery.com

7. THE APPLE FARM: 18501 Greenwood Road, Philo, CA 95466, +1 707.895.2333, www.philoapplefarm.com

8. LAUREN'S: 14211 Anderson Valley Highway, Boonville, CA 95415, +1 707.895.3869, www.laurensgoodfood.com

9. HENDY WOODS STATE PARK: 18599 Philo Greenwood Road, Philo, CA 95466, +1 707.895.3537, www.parks.ca.gov/?page_id=438

10. MOSSWOOD MARKET: 14111 Anderson Valley Highway, Boonville, CA 95415, +1 707. 895.3635, Facebook: The Mosswood Market

11. ANDERSON VALLEY BREWING COMPANY: 17700 Boonville Ukiah Road (CA-253), Boonville, CA 95415, +1 707.895.BEER (2337), www.avbc.com

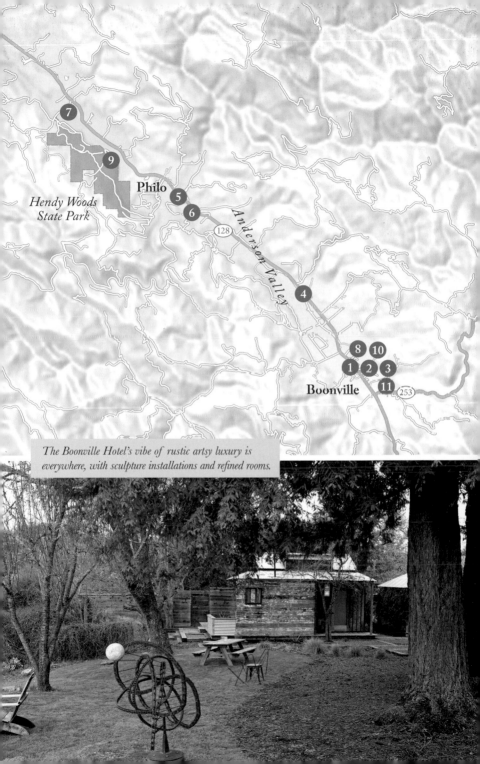

Hendy Woods
State Park

Philo

Anderson Valley

128

Boonville

253

The Boonville Hotel's vibe of rustic artsy luxury is everywhere, with sculpture installations and refined rooms.

11

Spring Back to Yourself • *Ukiah*

WHEN YOU LAND UPON HOT SPRINGS AS A DESTINATION, YOU ARE clearly looking for a specific kind of weekend retreat, one that is healing and peaceful and returns you to yourself. Even the drive to **Orr Hot Springs** on the outskirts of Ukiah begins to renew the spirit. Once you take a left onto Orr Springs Road, you are in the quiet – the kind of quiet that has depth and weight. The winding roads lead up to classic Northern California oak-strewn pastures and then back down into the wooded environs of the resort. Orr feels like the only thing for miles because it is.

Before you arrive, you will need to do a little preparation for your weekend. Food and beverages are not available at Orr, and as you'll discover on your drive, the closest shop is not that close. The compound includes a well-equipped communal kitchen in which to prepare your own meals. The process is both interactive and meditative, moving around with the other guests as you fix breakfast, discreetly admiring one another's oatmeal toppings or bacon. The **Natural Foods Co-Op** in downtown Ukiah will outfit you well. They have an extensive selection of prepared foods as well as a beautiful produce section and anything else you might need. If cooking is part of your idea of a relaxing weekend, set yourself up for some extraordinary meals here and enjoy. Once you arrive, you will be given bus tubs and name tags so you can store your food in the shared refrigerators and pantry.

> TIP: *Breakfast and dinner tend to be the busiest times in the kitchen. So if you like to have a lot of space to cook or will need several burners, try to eat a little earlier or later than the 9am and 6pm rushes.*

There are a few different room experiences at Orr. For the most privacy (and the longest walk to the baths and kitchen), there are yurts up on the hill, numbered 20 to 24. A couple of the larger accommodations come with a kitchen, a good option for families in particular. One of the most unique rooms is Number 1, which is draped in ivy and has taken on the feel of a hobbit dwelling. Despite a skylight, the interior is a little dark but very charming. If you are a camper, Orr is a lovely place to pitch your tent. For $60 a night, you can camp and enjoy all-day access to the baths and facilities.

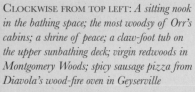

CLOCKWISE FROM TOP LEFT: *A sitting nook in the bathing space; the most woodsy of Orr's cabins; a shrine of peace; a claw-foot tub on the upper sunbathing deck; virgin redwoods in Montgomery Woods; spicy sausage pizza from Diavola's wood-fire oven in Geyserville*

On to the baths! There is not much else to do on the grounds but soak, which is just right for this weekend. Be advised that the baths are clothing optional and the tone is very respectful. Children are allowed but with some caveats – they must be accompanied by two adults and adhere to the general mellowness. If you are thinking about bringing kids, take a look at the policy page on Orr's website.

TIP: *Bathrobes and bath towels are available for rent but not provided, so bring your own towels, a cover-up, and comfortable shoes to get from your room to the baths and back.*

Business aside, the baths offer a full ceremonial experience. Once you enter the spa gates and walk over the creek, you will start out in the locker-lined changing area, which is right next to the massage rooms. Through the changing area are two hot tubs that are for all comers. The first and smaller of the two has a fountain that gushes in an intense rush and acts as a thorough shoulder massage. If you climb the wooden stairs to the deck above, you will find two claw-foot tubs, en plein air. Here you can set the water temp to suit yourself and get some sunshine, as well as a view of the lush grounds. Farther on is a large, cold spring-fed pool built into the hillside that's both long enough to take some laps and perfect for a plunge. The last rooms in the bath suite are a steam room and a dry sauna. If you prefer solitude or would like to stay out of the sun, there is a string of small chambers that each has its own claw-foot tub, a door that can be closed for privacy, and nothing else.

After a morning soak, a sun-dappled hike is in order. Pack up a picnic lunch from your provisions and set off on foot down Orr Springs Road. After a few minutes, you will be accompanied by a creek on the right and you can leave the road and walk alongside it for most of the journey. In 1.3 miles you will arrive at the entrance to **Montgomery Woods State Reserve**, a virgin redwood forest full of trails. If you follow the creek upstream, you will be led on a gentle three-mile walk through five redwood groves.

Back at Orr, you can partake in the indulgence of a second bathing session. The claw-foot tubs on the deck are the perfect place to stargaze before or after dinner (or both), as your body absorbs the mineral-rich waters springing straight from the earth.

The trip home to the big city is best taken at a leisurely pace so as not to re-knot those kinks you've spent all weekend unwinding. Geyserville is the halfway point and happens to be home to a restaurant that is a real find and a favorite of North Bay chefs. **Diavola Pizzeria & Salumeria** has a sunny deck for outdoor dining and makes an exemplary wood-burning-oven-prepared pizza. They also source ingredients from this land of milk and honey and make their own sausage and cured meats.

Once you reenter the atmosphere of daily life, you will be hardly recognizable, babtized as you are in the peaceful effervescence of Orr.

View from the road to Orr Hot Springs in Mendocino County.

Distance from San Francisco to Ukiah: *128 miles*
Drive time: *2 hours, 30 minutes*
Getting there: *US-101 N to North State St in Ukiah to Orr Springs Rd*

1. ORR HOT SPRINGS: 13201 Orr Spring Road, Ukiah, CA 95482, +1 707.462.6277, www.orrhotsprings.org, orrreservations@gmail.com
   Details: *Single rooms, cabins, yurts; $180–$250 per night. Camping sites available; $60 per night for camping. $30 for day use of baths. Weekends book up, so reserve ahead. Children must be accompanied by two adults. No pets.*

2. UKIAH NATURAL FOODS CO-OP: 721 South State Street, Ukiah, CA 95482, +1 707.462.4778, www.ukiahcoop.com

3. MONTGOMERY WOODS STATE RESERVE: 15825 Orr Springs Road, Ukiah, CA 95482, www.parks.ca.gov

4. DIAVOLA PIZZERIA & SALUMERIA: 21021 Geyserville Avenue, Geyserville, CA 95441, +1 707.814.0111, www.diavolapizzeria.com

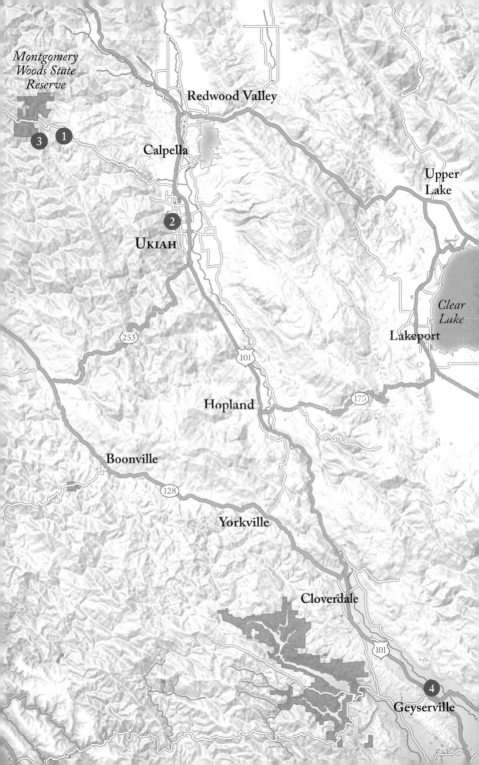

12

An Almost Unearthly Artists Colony • *Mendocino*

Towns have souls and needs like other living things. People forget this. When I first saw Mendocino, I became excited. It had an unusual, almost unearthly quality about it – pure, quiet, unsullied – but it was dying. I knew I could help it, help it get back on its feet and make it a place where people would get a simple but profound satisfaction out of living.

– Bill Zacha

THE LANDSCAPE OF MENDOCINO IS INSPIRING IN ITS PICTURESQUE brutality and it is no surprise that artists have long been drawn here, not just for the views but also for the quiet and for each other. The town is not just galleries and commerce, but a breathing, borderless artists colony.

Mendocino retains a feeling of the past in its present. Many of the homes and shops are from the 1800s and water towers hover above street level. But despite its appearance the town has not continuously thrived. Bill Zacha helped change that when he moved to Mendocino in the late 1950s and for $50 down, bought an old Victorian, which became the **Mendocino Art Center**. He also rallied residents to reinvest in buildings, opened a gallery/Laundromat, and taught art at Mendocino High School. They don't make men like Bill Zacha anymore, but then I don't know when men like Bill Zacha were ever really being mass-produced.

Approaching from the south, you will reach your hotel before you reach the town. **Little River Inn** has been owned by the same family for 75 years and it is truly one of the finest seaside lodgings in a strip of land perhaps more concentrated with fine inns than anywhere else in the country. There may be another that speaks to you more, but you won't find one that is warmer, cozier, lovelier than Little River. Cabins are outfitted with fireplaces and there is a nine-hole golf course and a stretch of beach perfect for a sunset amble. Dinner at the inn is a sweet end to the work week and the long drive that brought you here – classic Californian fine dining done with love. From the moment you arrive at Little River, you're already in the artistry of this coastal cloister.

Come Saturday morning, the Mendocino Art Center awaits you. Shows here are rotating and feature an impressive roster of international artists. There are also classes and frequent events. This is the creative center of the community and it is spoken of with reverence and joy.

Explore this building that continues to be a magnet for artists the world over and then head out to see what this magnet has drawn in.

Walk the couple of blocks to **Café Beaujolais**, which is a shining example of the category "restaurants in houses." Described by one local gallerist as "birthday food," it is an affordable splurge. The cafe is also a bakery and if you come after 4pm, when lunch service is over, you will walk through the garden to a window, where freshly baked bread is sold.

The afternoon is well spent drifting through town and exploring all of the galleries. Jewelry is another local artisan specialty and there are several fine jewelers, including Old Gold, which offers some classic designs you may recognize. **Mendocino Gems** is a seductive corner shop featuring an eclectic and colorful stone-centric collection of baubles. Owner Judith Beam has an on-site workbench and invites other jewelry makers to practice their craft there as well.

> TIP: *If you have time to drive the extra miles north, head to nature's gem shop, **Glass Beach**, in Fort Bragg. Sunset will show it in its best light. From the parking lot, it is a very short walk and a little climb down (just a few steps) to the shoreline.*

Slink along the coast back to Little River for dinner-as-art at **Wild Fish**, a seafood restaurant that prepares each meal with stunning attention to detail, each locally foraged ingredient smeared on the palette and painted on the plate, becoming a new thing – a celery soup with wild mussels, a sesame-encrusted sablefish, a chocolate mole pot de crème. Wild, sustainably caught fish is a rare thing and it often means the restaurant, like this one, has a special relationship with local fishermen, and you never know what might turn up on the menu. Sated and inspired, head back to your room to cozy up with a roaring fire and do as artists do – notice beauty, enjoy beauty, create beauty.

Morning in Mendocino starts at **Goodlife** for many local residents. You can do a full sit-down deal or grab a cup of coffee and a pastry and get back into town life. Or maybe you are the type of artist who starts their day at Leonard Moore Cannabis Cooperative, which boasts a "farmer-to-patient" ethos and shares all manifestations (edible, smokable, drinkable) of the crop that has long been a sideline industry for Mendocino County.

Highlight Gallery owns a precious bit of real estate along Main Street, which looks out on the water and feels like maybe the last block

You can sometimes see whale spouts in the Pacific right from Main Street in downtown Mendocino.

on Earth as it trails off. If you stand at the counter and look out the window you might be lucky enough to see whale spouts. The upstairs has enviable bay windows that frame the coast as if it were a possessable piece of art. Take in the paintings made of more than 100 shades of sand – works that evoke the vertiginous sensation of the tide pulling water back to the ocean from under your feet. The gallery has many regional and nationally known artists and has installed a room for local artists who have passed away, a sort of memorial to the concentrated talent of the county.

On the way out of town, stop at the most darling grocers in the whole universe, **Corners of the Mouth**, which is housed in an old church and is deliciously well stocked with natural chocolates and ripe fruit, and smells like health food stores used to smell. As you head home, pause at the southern cultural border of Mendocino for a last respite at the 136-year-old **Heritage House** resort and spa. Despite having passed through the hands of many owners, most of its classic grandeur survives in the great room, with its stunning fireplace and one of the most dramatic views in the area. Have a warm drink and take a picture of this place in the part of your mind that turns a memory into a work of art.

CLOCKWISE FROM TOP LEFT: *Salad Niçoise at Beaujolais; Main Street's gallery district; Little River Inn; water tower in downtown Mendocino* OPPOSITE: *Glass Beach in Fort Bragg.*

The town of Mendocino, perched above the shoreline of the Pacific Ocean.

Distance from San Francisco to Little River: *150 miles*
Drive time: *3 hours*
Getting there: *US-101 N to CA-128 W to CA-1 N*

1. LITTLE RIVER INN: 7751 Highway One, Little River, CA 95456, +1 707.937.5942, www.littleriverinn.com
   Details: *Three air-conditioned guest rooms; $189–$369 per night. Room service available.*

2. MENDOCINO ART CENTER: 45200 Little Lake Street, Mendocino, CA 95460, +1 707.937.5818, www.mendocinoartcenter.org

3. CAFÉ BEAUJOLAIS: 961 Ukiah Street, Mendocino, CA 95460, +1 707.937.5614, www.cafebeaujolais.com

4. MENDOCINO GEMS: 10483 Lansing Street, Mendocino, CA 95460, +1 707.409.0136, www.mendocinogems.com

5. GLASS BEACH: Elm Street & Old Haul Road, Fort Bragg, CA 95437, www.mendocino.com/glass-beach.html

6. WILD FISH: 7750 North Highway One, Little River, California 95456, +1 707.937.3055, www.wild-fish.com

7. GOODLIFE CAFÉ & BAKERY: 10483 Lansing Street, Mendocino, CA 95460, +1 707.937.0836, www.goodlifecafemendo.com

8. THE HIGHLIGHT GALLERY: 45094 Main Street, Mendocino, CA 95460, +1 707.937.3132, www.thehighlightgallery.com

9. CORNERS OF THE MOUTH: 45015 Ukiah Street, Mendocino, CA 95460, +1 707.937.5345, www.cornersofthemouth.com

10. THE HERITAGE HOUSE: 5200 Highway One, Little River, CA 95456, +1 707.202.9000, www.heritagehouseresort.com

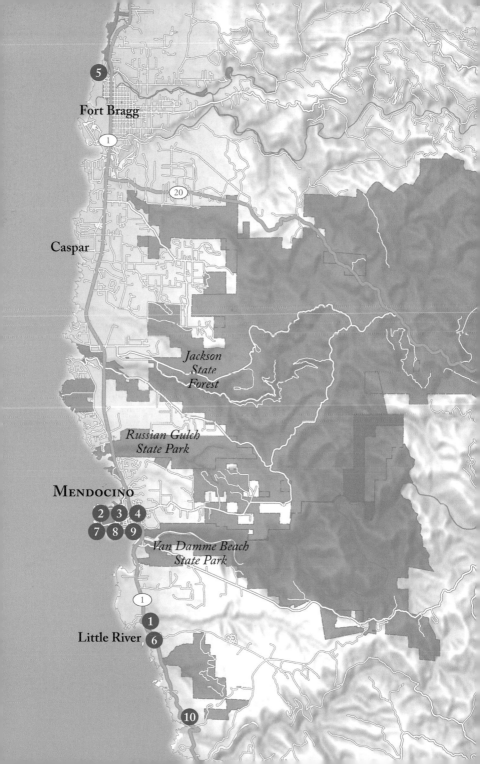

13

Literary Lookout · *Big Sur*

Big Sur is the California that men dreamed of years ago ... this is the face of the earth as the Creator intended it to look. – Henry Miller

IN THE REBELLIOUS AND DREAMY IDEALISM OF BEATNIK COUNTER-culture, **Big Sur** existed as one of the respites from spiritual and creative oppression. What do you find when you get in your car and drive to the end of the Earth, running from what dampened you? Freedom crashes into you and you're left a seeker, but sitting still. The northern portion of Big Sur is filled with the relics and retreats of artists past, as well as a multitude of spots where you might just start your novel or finish a haiku.

There are many ways to be a writer and not all of us are cut from the bohemian cloth. Perhaps you already have that screenplay under your belt and are ready to celebrate in style. **Post Ranch Inn** is a magnificent, if pricey, cloud in the heaven of Big Sur. And you may just run into some other stars here in the lofty atmosphere, as the hotel has long been an L.A. getaway. For good reason: a room with a moon roof, a luxurious tree house, and a hot tub overlooking the sea is just one combination of many options available.

If you are farther from the apex of your career or you favor a thinner membrane between you and the outside world, there is **Deetjen's Big Sur Inn and Restaurant**, an eccentric and sweet refuge for the creative, each room a different experience and feel. Deetjen's has its own cast of devotees, who come back each year to be in this quirky and cozy take on Big Sur. They also serve a tasty dinner with an eye toward local and organic ingredients.

The focal point of Big Sur literary history is the **Henry Miller Library**. Suited to a man who didn't believe in monuments, it is a humble cabin on a property he once inhabited when it was owned by his friend Emil White, whose mailbox still sits outside the front gate. The library has an excellent collection of books by one of America's own mirrors. For almost 20 years, Miller lived in Big Sur, at this place, which continues to be a lightning rod for oddballs and geniuses. At any time, a Big Surian salon is gathered on the library's front porch, discussing ideas, surrounded by art installations and the grassy stage. The Henry Miller Library is also a venue for concerts of notable singer-songwriters and bands, like the Flaming Lips and Rufus Wainwright. If an act you love

CLOCKWISE FROM TOP LEFT: *A cozy room at Deetjen's; breakfast at Big Sur Bakery; artist Jayson Fann's Spirit Nest; the original owner's mailbox at the Henry Miller Museum site; phoenix sculpture at Nepenthe*

is playing here, you should draw on your inner Neal Cassady and get on the road, because it is an intimate and unforgettable setting. On Sunday evenings there are open-mic poetry readings for the gutsy scribbler.

TIP: *If you forgot a good book and you've already made your way through Miller's oeuvre, you can purchase other authors here at this library/book shop and there is also the Big Sur Library on Highway One, just north of Glen Oaks Big Sur.*

Perhaps you're not the hole-up-in-your-hotel type of artist but more of the cafe swell. **Big Sur Bakery & Restaurant** is custom-made for a writerly day. There is fabulous coffee or wine – depending on the position of the sun, nourishing meals, and treats for when you get that first chapter on the page – peanut-butter-and-jelly cookies, bacon croissants, strawberry-and-brown-sugar streusel – you get the drift.

The bakery is surrounded by Loma Vista, which is a combination of performance venue, artists' studios, and residences that extend up the hill. Folk acts sometimes tour through here and play on the wooden outdoor stage. You will definitely run into the town's artist community, coming in for their morning macchiato or to catch up with the staff. And behind the cafe, you can spy some of the local artists' installations, such as the *Spirit Nests* of Jayson Fann.

TIP: *Big Sur Bakery puts out their bread every day at 9am and it is usually gone by 10am on the weekends, so get in line early if you hope to grab a loaf or a hot-from-the-oven slice.*

At **Nepenthe**, or "Isle of No Care," the Godlike nature of the creator may inhabit you. The fog tends to linger longest in this nook and it can feel as though you are floating above the clouds for much of the day. The view and the high-ceilinged architecture can give you a sense of soaring while also rooting you in the literary history of the community. The restaurant, which also houses the **Phoenix** store and a cafe, was once the grounds of Lolly and Bill Fassett's family home. Before this storied couple bought the property, a novelist named Lynda Sargent wrote and lived in the Log House, on the same strip of land, and gave shelter to Henry Miller, who continued to visit the Fassett family at "Nepenthe," as they called their residence, in his Big Sur years.

During the day, the umbrellaed terrace is the best place for a view of the marine layer's slow retreat and for a glass of wine and light lunch. In the evening, two fires compete for your attention. Inside the restaurant is a glorious fireplace in the round, which you can see from any of the tables along the perimeter or from the bar, a popular gathering spot. Outside, there is an enormous pit that has long been the terrain of big talkers and tale tellers. You may just find your next story while eavesdropping there. Though Nepenthe certainly fits the template of a "paying for the view" tourist trap, the food is straightforward and good and not at all an afterthought. And you can always pay a little less by having a martini and fries at the bar.

Miller loved to hike through the redwoods to get his blood pumping as inspiration and antidote to the typewriter. On the northern side of Big Sur National Park is **Julia Pfeiffer Burns State Park**, which is a robust site for the curious walker. Besides the redwoods, you will hike among willows, oaks, sycamores, and many other species, all shelter to a panoply of wildlife, including the banana slug, a good-luck omen. The Big Sur River moves through Julia Pfeiffer Burns on its way to the ocean. Plenty of fodder for your koans. Whether you are a writer or a lover of literature, you will certainly feel the churn of creation in Big Sur, the birthplace of more unfinished novels than perhaps anywhere else on Earth.

Rocky Creek Bridge on Highway One, as it weaves along the Big Sur coast.

Distance from San Francisco to Big Sur: *150 miles*
Drive time: *3 hours*
Getting there: *US-101 S to CA-156 W to CA-1 S*

1. POST RANCH INN: 47900 Highway One, Big Sur, CA 93920, +1 800.527.2200, www.postranchinn.com
   Details: *$775–$2500 per night. Breakfast included and can be served in your room.*

2. DEETJEN'S BIG SUR INN: 48865 Highway One, Big Sur, CA 93920, +1 831.667.2377, www.deetjens.com.
   Details: *$105–$290 per night. Less-expensive rooms have shared baths.*

3. THE HENRY MILLER LIBRARY: 48603 Highway One, Big Sur, CA 93920, +1 831.667.2574, www.store.henrymiller.org
   Details: *Open daily 11am–6pm, though occasionally closed for renovations. Check the website for details or events that might coincide with your visit.*

4. BIG SUR BAKERY: 47540 Highway One, Big Sur, CA 93920, +1 831.667.0520, www.bigsurbakery.com

5. LOMA VISTA GARDENS AND ARTISTS STUDIOS: 47540 Highway One, Big Sur, CA 93920, Facebook: Loma Vista Gardens

6. NEPENTHE: 48510 Highway One, Big Sur, CA 93920, +1 831.667.2345, www.nepenthebigsur.com

7. JULIA PFEIFFER BURNS STATE PARK: 47555 Highway One, Big Sur, CA 93920, +1 831.667.2315, www.parks.ca.gov

What are you waiting for?

14

Shangri-la for Your Inner Shaman • *Big Sur*

THERE IS NO BETTER PLACE ON EARTH TO DELVE INTO YOUR OWN depths than Big Sur. It is impossible to not shed 20 pounds directly off of your shoulders when you take in the operatic views of the Pacific, or wander among the redwoods. Big Sur is awash in sacred sanctuaries to elevate body and soul. You begin to feel it the moment Highway One hugs the coastline, but it really hits you when you enter Big Sur National Park and the mountains and ocean spectacularly come together. From the sweeping views to the majestic New Deal-era bridges, you will be thankful there are many vista points to pull over and take it all in. And when sunset hits, it is mandatory that you stop whatever you are doing and find a place where you can silently gaze out over the water.

Esalen is a legendary retreat center and wellness mecca. Its name is invoked as shorthand for a kind of getaway that speaks to body, mind, and spirit. The Esalen experience is grounded in two roots: environment and transformation. If you are looking purely for a hotel, there are many special ones in Big Sur, but if it's healing and inner growth you're seeking, Esalen is the sanctum sanctorum.

TIP: *If you're interested in carpooling to Esalen, let the resort know, and they'll do their best to pair you up with another guest.*

Esalen is perched on a cliff's edge in Big Sur, putting the scenery constantly on view. Crack your window at night to hear the waves crashing, take a stroll to the silent meditation yurt and smell the woods, or lounge in the hanging swing bed to take in the magnificent sights of sea and sky. And, really, magnificent only hints at the beauty. You even absorb the environment in the delicious and simple food enjoyed in the group setting of Esalen's cafeteria, as much of it is grown right on the property in the retreat's verdant gardens. Perhaps the deepest environmental plunge is in the mineral baths, mostly clothing optional. Well known among hot-spring junkies, these waters have been healing visitors since the late 1800s. All the pools look out over the Pacific. The bathhouse, with its individual claw-foot tubs fed by thermal waters – which can be adjusted to your temperature preference – is a glorious spot to wind down and do some stargazing after a full day of inner growth.

You must be an overnight guest at Esalen to be on the grounds, and there are a few ways to stay. The simplest is to sign up for a personal retreat, which means you have a private room and full run of the facilities without participating in a workshop.

Many also choose to sign up for one of the workshops offered (more than 600 every year), in subjects ranging from shamanism to yoga to writing and beyond, led by experts who come from all over the world to share their knowledge. These classes keep you busy for a large chunk of the day but leave plenty of time to just "be." There are also optional group activities at the edges of the days – dancing, yoga, meditation, and others, depending on the week. Esalen is designed to offer ample opportunities for personal transformation. Whether your journey takes you through upheaval and discovery in a spirituality workshop or through stillness, you are supported. The support comes in the form of nourishing food, lots of space to be quiet and reflective, and a warm staff.

One of the sweet things about Esalen is its ethic to make space available to as many people as possible. If you can't afford a private room, there are much cheaper options if you are willing to sleep in a bunk bed or sleeping bag in a group room. You can also make work/trade arrangements with the staff. Once you're there, regardless of the sleeping accommodation, it is Shangri-la.

The meals are served during windows of a few hours to come and choose from a hearty selection. While Esalen is not vegetarian, the options are vegetable- and grain-based, so you might want to smuggle in some jerky if you need animal protein.

> TIP: *The baths are least crowded during mealtimes. If you eat early and then head down to the bathhouse while others are still lingering over their food, you will likely get a tub with no waiting.*

A meditative moment at Esalen, where there are abundant nooks to sit, think, and take in the beauty.

CLOCKWISE FROM TOP LEFT: *Welcome to Esalen; last chance for gas in Big Sur; contemplative spot at New Camaldoli Hermitage; mini waterfall in Limekiln State Park; Loma Vista Buddha* OPPOSITE: *Bixby Bridge disappears in the fog along Highway One.*

If you want to soak in the Esalen baths without staying overnight, there is one exception to their "guests only" rule: you can come between 1am and 3am by calling ahead and reserving one of the 20 spots available each night (+1 831.667.3047).

Another stop on the monastic path of Big Sur is the **New Camaldoli Hermitage**, where the monks take a vow of silence and also make fantastic fruitcake, available at the gift shop. Some of their other offerings are Mystic Monks Coffee and Holy Granola. Who says the pious can't pun? The chapel, which has daily services, and the gift shop are at the top of a wildly scenic two-mile drive (or very steep hike). This retreat center is higher up off the coastline than Esalen and has a more spacious, arid microclimate. Park at the peak, grab some granola and wander for a while. There are comfortable benches at most vistas, so you can absorb the grace.

Sometimes the deeper truths can only be found on the path you forge yourself. **Limekiln State Park** is a wonderful place to look for them. There are a few camping sites available, or it is ideal for a walkabout. If you go up the hill, you will follow a forested path to a waterfall or fork off toward the limekilns, where much of the lime used in San Francisco was mined and extracted from 1887 to 1890. If it's the sea you crave, you can go downhill and find a short but deep stretch of beach, with soft sand and some picnic tables.

> TIP: *Fuel up on your way out of town at the only gas station for 40 miles (17540 California One, Big Sur, CA 93920) and possibly the cutest one you've ever seen. (There are three gas stations in Big Sur. The station farthest south is in front of Big Sur Bakery and the station farthest north is just after Glen Oaks Big Sur.)*

To take a bit of cheeky esoterica with you, pull into the lot at Big Sur Bakery and Restaurant. Past the wooden gate to the left is a closet shop called the **Altar**, with art-cum-souvenirs made by the owners. Screen-printed T-shirts of the Madonna, tiny hexes for your enemies, and hot pink rabbit-foot accessories allow you to take home your inner peace with a wink.

The pocket beach at Limekiln State Park has a few camping spots, if you want to extend your stay.

Distance from San Francisco to Big Sur: *150 miles*
Drive time: *3 hours*
Getting there: *US-101 S to CA-156 W to CA-1 S*

1. THE ESALEN INSTITUTE: 55000 Highway One, Big Sur, CA 93920, +1 888.837.2536, www.esalen.org, info@esalen.org
   Details: *Single rooms, cabins, yurts, and group sleeping options available, 125 beds total; $130–$725 per person, per night. More than 600 workshops offered each year. No pets.*

2. NEW CAMALDOLI HERMITAGE BAKERY & GIFT STORE: 62475 Highway One, Big Sur, CA 93920, www.hermitagebigsur.com

3. LIMEKILN STATE PARK: Highway One, Big Sur, CA 93920, www.parks.ca.gov, +1 805.434.1996

4. THE ALTAR: 47540 Highway One, Big Sur, CA 93920, +1 831.238.2828; Facebook: The Altar: Big Sur

15

The Yin of Napa · *Napa Valley*

YIN: female principle of the universe, characterized as sustaining and associated with earth, darkness, and mystery.

THE YIN QUALITIES OF NAPA ARE THE FLEETING COMPLEXITIES OF flavor in a perfectly executed vintage, and growing styles that honor quality over profit. These are the roots that draw the deepest waters of Napa's character – the relationship to the land and the expression of that terroir that continue to drive some of the world's finest winemakers. A few days of Napa yin will enfold you in this relationship and all the satellite passions of those who nurture the vine.

Start the weekend by immersing yourself in Napa's most celebrated non-vinous preoccupation: food. At the restaurant **Torc**, chef Sean O'Toole's kitchen sends out dishes that are so beautifully plated and prepared with such care, it feels like you must be the only person in the restaurant. A roast chicken served with a bouquet of wildflowers and herbs, absolutely definitive risotto, pumpkin soup with black trumpet mushrooms and Hobb's bacon are examples of a continually rotating menu tuned to the seasonal moods of the valley.

After dinner, settle into your haven of yin: **Bardessono** in Yountville is like an eco-luxury spaceship, floating on its own plane of radiant peacefulness in the heart of downtown. Indoor/outdoor showers that transform into steam rooms with the push of a button, poolside cabanas that close for complete privacy and open for cocktail service, and a fleet of black Lexus SUVs to chauffeur you around town all conspire to make you feel as wealthy as you may or may not be.

It may be hard to leave this otherworldly oasis in the morning, but if you can, amble down to **Bouchon Bakery**, where notorious culinary perfectionist Thomas Keller has honed his pastries to meta-Frenchness. A café au lait and pain au raisin will begin a grape-filled day quite nicely.

> TIP: *En route to your first tasting (at Corison), stop in at* **Oakville Grocery** *and grab some lunch to enjoy on the winery's terrace. Better yet, go online (www.oakvillegrocery.com) and order a picnic (crab-cake sandwich with bacon, red pepper relish, and avocado, maybe) to be ready when you arrive.*

CLOCKWISE FROM TOP LEFT: *Corison Winery vines; Chappallet's "artful" tasting room; Bouchon Bakery pastries; welcome to Bardessono; Mumm Napa bubbly; first course at Torc*

Farther north along Saint Helena Highway, you will find **Corison**. Cathy Corison's organic wines are made with a thoughtfulness separate from the industry of wine; they are a "snapshot of nature," in the words of their trade coordinator, Justin Boudrie. They make only Cabernet Sauvignon, a specialty of the Rutherford appellation, showing that wines from this region can still speak in "a pure, restrained voice without artifice or bombast," as *New York Times* wine critic Eric Asimov said. Appointments to taste from their library, which start on the hour from 10am to 4pm, are necessary. The Kronos Cab is made only from the grapes growing right behind the tasting room and expresses the long narrative of some of the oldest vines in Napa.

Saunter south to downtown Napa for dinner. **Ninebark** is owned by famed commercial-space designers AvroKo and is a magnificent upgrade of an old bar that closed years ago, with classic Napa brick walls. There is a hip downstairs bar, but on the third floor is a rooftop bar with a view of the Napa River, the coolest place in town to have something other than wine. Try one of their house-made bottled cocktails, like a refreshing Pomona. Head to the middle floor for your dinner reservation and enjoy the intricate lightness of two-Michelin-starred chef Matthew Lightner's cooking. Call Bardessono to pick you up after dinner and have a nightcap in their elegant and convivial lounge before slumber.

Sunday morning, after duck confit hash with a duck egg sunny-side up in the hotel's Lucy Restaurant, amble over to your spa appointment for a "Vinotherapy" treatment, an anti-aging massage that uses Chardonnay grape-seed oil to peel away years – and the wine-soaked night before. Or for an even more personalized pampering, engage a spa butler to come to your room and draw a seasonally specific bath served up with a glass of sparkling wine to keep you company.

Keep your morning champagne buzz going: towel off and wind your way up the Silverado Trail, Napa's most beautiful and iconic thoroughfare, to **Mumm**'s, maker of sparkling wines that are world renowned. The tasting, situated in a glass room hovering above the estate's expansive vineyard, feels like a ladies' luncheon.

TIP: *Bring some sandwiches, like a Parisian ham and Emmenthaler cheese on baguette, from Bouchon Bakery, and you can have the world's most civilized picnic with your sparkling service.*

Whether you sample the bubbles or not, you can take in Mumm's fine-art photography gallery, with changing exhibitions. Here you'll find dynamic museum-quality works, like a collection of Ansel Adams landscapes or Jim Marshall's iconic classic rock images. Begin a day of tasting with effervescence: the breakfast of wines, sparkling white.

Find your way next to the weekend's apex of yin: **Chappellet Winery** is one of the most visually stimulating tours in the valley, from their perch on Pritchard Hill, which they urged into an appellation. Since the 1960s, Donn Chappellet, his wife, Molly, and their six children have been defining the art of land stewardship as well as enology. An Edward Moses-designed pyramid winery building filled with art (much of it by Donn and Molly's daughter Lygia), a "boulder garden" of rocks removed from their vineyards, and installations of tumbleweed-like masses of rusted wire are some of the ways that the pragmatic becomes the transcendent at Chappellet.

High marks are consistent for all of their wines; the Chenin Blanc is so sought after that it's hard to find, and the estate Cabernet Sauvignon is remarkable. Make an appointment for a tasting to celebrate a relationship with land that has grown deeper, rather than wider, in its 50 years as a winery.

A lot of money and attention have poured into the Napa Valley, as more and more wine pours out of it. Even so, there are still many authentic winemakers that let the land speak its own truth, through the grapes. And if you walk away from the noise, you can hear its whisper.

What are you waiting for?

Distance from San Francisco to Napa: *55 miles*
Drive time: *1 hour, 15 minutes*
Getting there: *I-80 E to CA-37 West to CA-29 N*

1. BARDESSONO HOTEL & SPA: 6526 Yount Street, Yountville, CA 94599, +1 707.204.6000, www.bardessono.com
   Details: *$400–$1100 per night, depending on season and room type. Two-night minimum on weekends. LEED Platinum Certified Hotel with fireplaces, a la carte breakfast, and spa amenities.*

2. TORC: 1140 Main Street, Napa, CA 94559, +1 707.252.3292, www.torcnapa.com

3. BOUCHON BAKERY: 6528 Washington Street, Yountville, CA 94599, +1 707.944.2253, www.bouchonbakery.com

4. OAKVILLE GROCERY: 7856 Saint Helena Highway, Oakville, CA 94562, +1 707.944.8802, www.oakvillegrocery.com

5. CORISON WINERY: 987 Saint Helena Highway, Oakville, CA 94574, +1 707.963.0826, www.corison.com

6. NINEBARK: 813 Main Street, Napa, CA 94559, +1 707.226.7821, www.ninebark-napa.com

7. MUMM NAPA: 8445 Silverado Trail, Napa, CA 94558, +1 707.967.7700, mummnapa.com

8. CHAPPELLET WINERY: 1581 Sage Canyon Road, St. Helena, CA 94574, +1 707.286.4219, www.chappellet.com

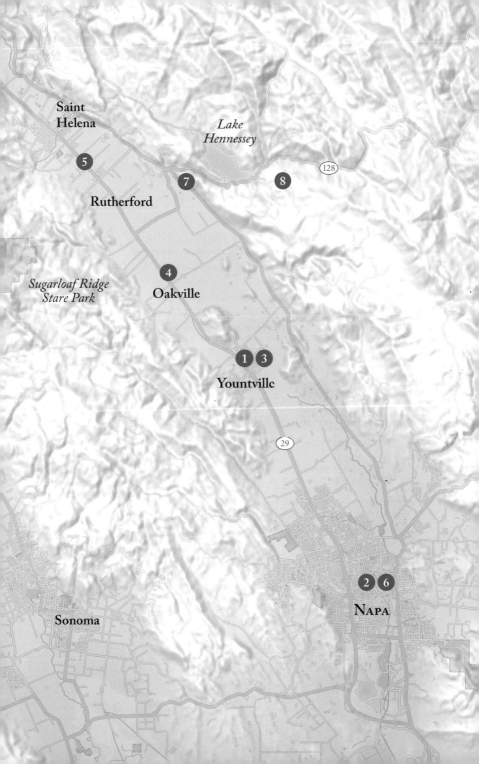

16

The Yang of Napa · *Napa Valley*

YANG: masculine active principle in nature that in Chinese cosmology is exhibited in light, heat, or dryness and that combines with yin to produce all that is.

WITH VELVETY, ROBUST WINES AND PALATIAL ARCHITECTURAL VISIONS, Napa has the intensity of Las Vegas combined with the open-eyed pragmatism of an ag town. Winemaking is farming, after all. Fabulous farming. Spend a weekend celebrating the yang of Napa's flavors, experiences, and sights – the muscular and straightforward qualities.

Poetry Inn concierges your weekend with an innkeeper all to yourself, view-drenched private patios, and fitness equipment brought to your room upon request. Each of the five guest rooms is named for an American poet; choose your favorite or book the whole place, if you travel as a pack. Outside the rooms are a pool, Jacuzzi, spa room, and a cellar fully stocked with Lede Family Wines, the owners of the property. The Robert Louis Stevenson Suite has an outdoor shower facing the sunrise.

Friday night, make your way to **Ca' Momi Osteria**, a big-hearted, passionate Italian eatery in Napa with not once but twice authenticated Napoletana pizza (VPN & APN), as well as Napa-glossed Italian classics from Veneto-born chef and co-owner Valentina Guolo-Migotto. She is as equally wild about offal as she is about obscure types of radicchio, and all of it goes with wine. After all, Ca' Momi started as a winemaking venture, then added a few little snacks to go with the wines (the enoteca is still thriving at Oxbow Market), and finally bloomed into a full-scale restaurant. The spirited food and atmosphere will surely fire up your chi.

> TIP: *If you like a good dive-bar nightcap, wet your whistle at* **Pancha's of Yountville**, *a salty and smoky saloon that serves strong, no-frills drinks – an antidote to all the "Napacity."*

Enjoy a three-course breakfast at Poetry Inn before heading out for a day in St. Helena. Your first stop is a tasting room that feels like a clubhouse for the peloton. **Velo Vino** is the public-facing space of Clif Family Winery, the same Clifs who make those bars tucked in your riding kit. Arrange to take one of their many cycling tours to match

your scenery proclivities, drinking goals, and fitness level. They will set you up with an espresso drink, bike rental, and itinerary and let you loose. When you return, you are welcome to a tasting and a snack from their definitely-not-a-roach-coach food truck. Tastings are more personal than most in Napa – choose a flight or select any one of the open bottles, a 2-ounce or 4-ounce pour. Start with the lightest of the bigs, their Rosé of Grenache, fruit-forward and dry and only produced in small quantities at Vino Velo. Snatch up a bottle or two.

TIP: *In case your ride burned more calories than the food truck replenished, you happen to be right down the street from one of the most famous burger stands in the state: Gott's Roadside. Formerly Taylor's Refresher, the sign and the quality remain. The milk shakes are so thick, they are a dare to the average straw. The line can be daunting but it moves fast, and the vibe is convivial – a buzzed and friendly crowd waiting together.*

After lunch, take in the colossal fantasy of V. Sattui's **Castello di Amorosa**. Fourth-generation winemaker Dario Sattui has transformed the vineyard's crest into a 107-room monument to medieval revelry: a 13th-century-style Tuscan castle, complete with a moat, dining hall, pigsty, and slightly tipsy looking suit of armor. There is even a torture chamber with an iron maiden. Sattui imported more than 800,000 bricks from the Old Country. The wines are almost beside the point here. Almost. An array of opportunities from a self-guided tour to a VIP experience with the house sommelier are all available, as are Castello wines that you can't find anywhere outside this authentically inauthentic Italian village.

Go from a palace to a palatial greenhouse-like space: **Press** in Saint Helena is Napa's chicest steakhouse and your dinner destination. While they don't bill it as such, they have several cuts of USDA Prime on the menu as well as grass-fed and Wagyu beef, and offer a la carte options, much like a classic casa de carne. When you are inundating yourself in the Cabs of this robust region, you need a meal that can hold its own. A dry-aged rib eye steak au poivre ought to give your glass a run for its money.

Day two: what could be more yangy than waking up to rock 'n' roll and red wine? After breakfast and a swim at the inn, the last tasting brings you full circle, to **Cliff Lede Vineyards**, which pairs wine and song in their Howard Backen-designed tasting room – in a renovated 1913 Craftsman-style bungalow – and outdoor gardens. Take the premium tour and have the tastes paired with a playlist selection. Like the rooms at Poetry Inn, the fields are named after classic tunes, and you can purchase a Marshall amp as well as a wine club subscription here. Their Stags Leap District Cabernets are inky and fruity and built to last. The highly rated wines are hard to find and worth splurging on at the winery.

CLOCKWISE FROM TOP LEFT: *Wine knight at Castello di Amorosa; Fatted Calf jerky; Vino Velo tasting; Cliff Lede names its vineyards after famous tunes; Gott's Roadside's juicy burger*

CLIFF LEDE VINEYARDS

Your Song

As you drive home to whatever energetic balance awaits you, stop at Napa's **Oxbow Market** and find the retail arm of Five Dot Ranch, owned by a seventh-generation ranching family. The butcher case features cuts of their beef, and their counter-service lunch offers a you-pick-it, we-grill-it meal. Choose the thickest, most marbled, dry-aged New York strip and add on extra-cheesy mac and cheese and roasted brussels sprouts with tomato-bacon jam. Continue on the carnivore's trail with a visit to Fatted Calf, a butcher shop plus. Stock up on house-made charcuterie, like ciciolli, spreadable confit of pork, and their addictive beef jerky. If bold meats require a denouement of bold sweets, Oxbow is also host to Three Twins Ice Cream, providing an opportunity to find out how a scoop of Dad's Cardamom tastes next to Banana Nut Confetti.

What is most profoundly yang in Napa can be taken home wrapped in butcher paper and in a case of bottles filled with sun and earth and audacity.

What are you waiting for?

Distance from San Francisco to Napa: *55 miles*
Drive time: *1 hour, 15 minutes*
Getting there: *I-80 E to CA-37 W to CA-29 N*

1. **Poetry Inn:** 6380 Silverado Trail, Napa, CA 94558, +1 707.944.0650, www.poetryinn.com
   Details: *Five rooms with twice-daily housekeeping, personalized concierge, spa services, three-course breakfast, and vineyard views; $650–$1100 per night.*

2. **Ca' Momi Osteria:** 1141 First Street, Napa, CA 94559, +1 707.224.6664, www.camomi.com

3. **Velo Vino:** 709 Main Street, St. Helena, CA 94574, +1 707.301.7188, www.cliffamilywinery.com

4. **Gott's Roadside:** 933 Main Street, St. Helena, CA 94574, +1 707.963.3486, www.gotts.com

5. **Castello di Amorosa:** 4045 St. Helena Highway, Calistoga, CA 94515, +1 707.967.6272, www.castellodiamorosa.com

6. **Press:** 587 St. Helena Highway, St. Helena, CA 94574, +1 707.967.0550, www.pressnapavalley.com

7. **Pancha's of Yountville :** 6764 Washington Street, Yountville, CA 94599, +1 707.944.2125

8. **Cliff Lede Vineyards:** 1473 Yountville Cross Road, Yountville, CA 94599, +1 707.944.8642, www.cliffledevineyards.com

9. **Oxbow Public Market :** 610 & 644 First Street, Napa, CA 94559 +1 707.226.6529, www.oxbowpublicmarket.com

Calistoga

5

(128)

Saint
Helena

Bothe-Napa Valley
State Park   4
          3
          6

Rutherford

1

8

Sugarloaf Ridge
Stare Park

7

Annadel
Stare Park   Kenwood

Yountville

(29)

Glen Ellen

Sonoma   2 9

                                          Napa

Castello di Amorosa's medieval-style towers and
ramparts have an imposing presence in Napa.

17

Dirty Luxury • *Calistoga & St. Helena*

MAINTAINING A SENSE OF ORDER AND CIVILITY TO EVERY INCH OF life can be exhausting. Truly carefree moments – the kind that often populate childhood – can be rare. The adult version of running amok in the backyard is a weekend at **Indian Springs Resort and Spa** in Calistoga, one of Napa County's more laid-back enclaves and a place known for its mud and steam.

When you roll into Calistoga on Friday night, stop at the informal town welcome wagon, **Buster's Original Southern Barbecue**, which is positioned right under the old-school light-up sign that points you to downtown from a four-way stop. A crossroads is a mythological place to summon the devil, and you will find some demonic elements here – smoking coals and red-hot sauce. Buster's is Texas style, so the brisket is a specialty. Start indulging in the liberating messiness of the weekend to come, and slather the meat in their flavorful elixir – they are known for their sauces. If it's warm enough, take your plate out to the recently upgraded outdoor seating area, which feels a little removed from the Sturm und Drang of the grills and the ever-long line. Belly full and fingers licked, head to your room at Indian Springs in a meaty haze.

> TIP: *Though check-in isn't until 3pm, you can use the beloved pools at Indian Springs from 11am as a guest. If you can play hooky on Friday, head up early and take advantage of this generous policy.*

Indian Springs is an old-world spa meant to soak you in the healing properties of volcanic-ash mud and mineral water, collected right on the property from an active geyser. You can stay in the main hotel, an old Hollywood Spanish-style lodge, or one of the satellite dwellings, which range from the original historical cottages to modern houses. The cottages are outfitted with kitchens and have access to shared grills, so you can come with friends and have a larger communal experience.

If you are staying in a room with a kitchenette, stop on the drive up at Santa Rosa's Sebastopol Road, the main artery of unincorporated Roseland, and a treasure trove of taquerias. **El Favorito** is a particular favorito and their quesadilla suiza is an untidy, decadent conglomeration of cheese, avocado, tortilla, and a meat of your choice. Make sure to ask for extra green salsa. Around the corner you will find **Lola's Market**,

CLOCKWISE FROM TOP LEFT: *Downtown St. Helena; messy and meaty at Buster's; mineral bath at Indian Springs; the Buddha Pond*

a regional chain of grocery stores specializing in Hispanic foodstuffs. Their deli has top-notch Mexican staples like guacamole, carnitas, and fresh pico de gallo. Why cook when you can simply assemble?

Indian Springs is a wine-country institution and a destination for detangling. Make a reservation for a mud bath when you book your room, especially if you want to ensure that you can get an appointment at the same time as another guest. The experience is not precious but that's part of the appeal. After you disrobe, you are rerobed in terrycloth and ushered to a concrete tub filled with hot, thick, mineral-rich mud. The sensation of sinking into the mud is both exhilarating and womblike. Once covered from toes to chin, an attentive staff member lays a cooling cloth over your eyes as you lie back and let the mud seep into your pores. If you are sensitive to heat, try keeping an arm above the surface. The process takes all of ten minutes to detoxify and stupefy.

After you emerge from the tub shellacked in shiny sludge, next comes a shower, followed by a geyser-water bath, where you receive all the tools needed to remove the mud from every nook or cranny. You can interlude in a mineral steam room scented with eucalyptus and lavender, if you aren't too wobbly kneed. Last, you are cocooned in flannel in a chamber of relaxation. If being buried in mud pushes a claustrophobic button, you can always go straight to the mineral bath and everything that follows.

TIP: *Post mud-and-mineral-bath, you can extend the spa experience and draw further from the Indian Springs well with a massage or facial. Or just take your tranquility to the Buddha, or at least to his large likeness, which overlooks a garden refuge with a pond, where chaise longues, a fireplace, and beverages meet your every little need.*

The rest of your afternoon needn't take you off Indian Springs' property. The Olympic-size 80-degree-plus mineral-water pool is hard to leave. The resort has a second, adults-only, pool, as well, which is quieter, smaller, and lit in the evening. Both pools are open until midnight, and swimming after dark is bound to make you feel like a kid again, even if you didn't have to sneak into the pool to use it.

Make yourself dinner in your bungalow from Lola's booty or drive down the road to the neighboring town of Saint Helena, with its picturesque Main-Street vibe and wine-country glamour. **Farmstead** is one of many standout restaurants to choose from, made more special as it is owned by the Long Meadow Ranch Winery, which grows much of its own meat and produce. If the evening is warm, you can sit outside among the grapevines while you enjoy thoughtful dishes like grass-fed beef short ribs served with greens, Vella cheddar grits, and barbeque sauce.

A slow Sunday beckons you back to Saint Helena for breakfast at **Model Bakery**. They've been around for more than 100 years for a reason – and the reason might just be their homemade English muffins. Order a breakfast sandwich and a latte and absorb the local color. Next to Model is **Woodhouse Chocolates**, an elegant maker of exquisite confections displayed like fine jewels. Follow your curiosity through the town's well-appointed shops, like **Ottoman Art**, a hall of Turkish delights – handbags, ceramics, and intricate boots, all arranged with artful intensity. Leave time on the drive home to San Francisco to stop at **Old Faithful Geyser**, a sight that has been eliciting mellow awe for hundreds of years, though these days with some added amenities. Every 20 to 30 minutes, the geyser erupts a few hundred feet into the air for a minute or two. The anticipation draws you into conversation with the other seekers. The owners have created shaded cabanas, bocce courts, liberal rules about wine consumption, and even a small petting zoo, welcoming you to linger indefinitely.

When you're ready to get back behind the wheel, don't tap the dust off your shoes – take home a little of the healing, calming, detoxifying dirt as a reminder that the best weekends can get a little messy.

Distance from San Francisco to Calistoga: *75 miles*
Drive time: *1 hour, 30 minutes*
Getting there: *US-101 N to Mark West Springs Rd*

1. INDIAN SPRINGS: 1712 Lincoln Avenue, Calistoga, CA 94515 +1 707.942.4913, www.indianspringscalistoga.com
   Details: *$250–$1200 per night, includes pool usage. Spa packages available separately.*

2. BUSTER'S SOUTHERN BBQ: 1207 Foothill Boulevard, Calistoga, CA 94515 +1 707.942.5605, www.busterssouthernbbq.com

3. TAQUERIA EL FAVORITO: 565 Sebastopol Road, Santa Rosa, CA 95407, +1 707.526.7444

4. LOLA'S MARKET: 440 Dutton Avenue #17, Santa Rosa, CA 95407 +1 707.577.8846, www.lolasmarkets.com

5. FARMSTEAD: 738 Main Street, St. Helena, CA 94574, +1 707.963.4555, www.longmeadowranch.com/Farmstead

6. THE MODEL BAKERY: 1357 Main Street, St. Helena, CA 94574, +1 707.963.8192, www.themodelbakery.com

7. WOODHOUSE CHOCOLATES: 1367 Main Street, St. Helena, CA 94574, +1 707.963.8413, www.woodhousechocolate.com

8. OTTOMAN ART: 1228 Main Street, St. Helena, CA 94574, +1 707.963.9300, Twitter: @OttomanArts

9. OLD FAITHFUL GEYSER: 1229 Tubbs Lane, Calistoga, CA 94515, +1 707.942.6463, www.oldfaithfulgeyser.com

Old Faithful's 1pm show reaching its steamy apex in Calistoga. Crowds gather every half hour to watch.

18

The Lake People • *Lake Berryessa, Napa & Fairfield*

SOME PEOPLE ARE LAKE PEOPLE. AND IF YOU ARE WONDERING IF YOU are, then you likely are not, because you must invest in some serious toys to be a Lake Person. You need at least a Jet Ski. And if you have a Jet Ski, then you need a truck to haul it and a place to store it and this is only the beginning. Of course, anyone can jump in the lake and enjoy it but that doesn't make you one of the tribe. You can, however, rent the toys and join in the good times on Lake Berryessa, Napa County's largest lake and a reservoir that provides water to San Francisco. A houseboat will get you in league with the lifetime lake folk and it will simplify your weekend in the nicest way.

En route to your floating castle, make one meal easy on yourself (this is a vacation, after all) and stop at a gem hidden in Val's Liquors: **Clemente's Authentic Italian Takeout**. Clemente Cittoni has been making ravioli and malfatti (literally translates as "badly made") – which are basically the insides of ravioli without the dough pillowcases – since the 1970s, when he emigrated from Lake Como. After having a restaurant for many years, he has pared down the operation to a take-out window. You place your order and then pay at the register next to the lottery tickets and tiny bottles of Bacardi, collecting your bowl of sugo-soaked, completely addictive little dumplings. They make plenty of other things too, but don't leave without the malfatti.

> TIP: *For the weekend's groceries, there are some markets on the way to the lake, but you might want to do your shopping on your home turf to prepare more completely. Also, remember you will have to carry everything you bring on and off the boat, including trash. Save yourself some hassle and go easy on the packing.*

Known for its Petit Sirah, Suisun Valley has been an AVA just one year less than Napa Valley and is home to many wineries. On the drive to Berryessa, you will pass the center of commerce for this appellation, an oasis along a stretch of country roads and vines. Stop at **Vezér Family Winery** for their ATV tour of the estate, where you will see the process unfold from the field to the glass. The excursion ends in the barrel room, where they show you how to make a blend. Grab a few bottles of their Cassie Petite Sirah to complement your ravioli in red sauce.

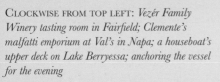

CLOCKWISE FROM TOP LEFT: *Vezér Family Winery tasting room in Fairfield; Clemente's malfatti emporium at Val's in Napa; a houseboat's upper deck on Lake Berryessa; anchoring the vessel for the evening*

As you near the lake, notice the abundant lace lichen gilding the oak trees. **Pleasure Cove** is the nerve center of activities on Berryessa. This is where you will rent your houseboat and where you gas it up. Three sizes of houseboat (59, 60, and 70 feet) are available; the two smaller boats sleep ten and the largest sleeps twelve and has a hot tub on the top deck. All the boats come equipped with a grill and kitchen facilities – oh, and a slide from the top deck that drops you into the water. That's just standard.

Houseboats absolutely force you to be quiet and un-busy, though there is much you can do on the lake. Fishing is big on Berryessa, with catfish, Chinook and kokanee salmon, brown and rainbow trout, smallmouth and largemouth bass, spotted bass, and blue gill aplenty, especially along the side channels. You can pull over on the north end of the lake to find walking trails that hug the shoreline and offer sightings of osprey, pelicans, and bald eagles. Swimming is luscious, especially in summer when the water is as warm as 75 degrees.

TIP: *If you are at Berryessa when the lake is full, find the Glory Hole spillway on the southeast side of the Monticello Dam, a bell-shaped drain that drops overflow into Putah Creek. This phenomenal site is thought to be the largest of its kind in the world.*

Jet Skis (WaveRunners or Sea-Doos, as they're more properly called) are available at **Lake Berryessa Boat & Jet Ski Rental** in Markley Cove. In fact, a small vessel like this can come in handy to scout your nightly parking spot. Boating is not allowed at night, so you will have to find a docking point and anchor the boat into the sand.

After disembarking, you'll still have some good daylight left. Head into Napa proper before you leave the county. Another delightful way to spend time on the water is by stand-up paddling. Napa's **High Water SUP** will cruise you along the gentle Napa River and provide a core workout. You can rent the paddleboards and head out on your own if you are already handy with this type of vessel, or take a 60-minute lesson. Owner Heather Bailie and her instructors also offer fusion classes that combine paddleboarding with yoga or fitness coaching, adding elements of balance and beauty to the sport.

Afterward, try some Italian ice cream at **Frati Gelato**, with river views from their patio.

TIP: *The Napa riverfront is teeming with great restaurants. If you want to linger for a meal, take a stroll down Main Street and find a place that suits your appetite – Zuzu (tapas), Ninebark (American farm to table), and Morimoto Napa (Japanese), to name a few.*

Sun kissed and water woozy, return home a member of the Lake People and the River People and the People Who Know How to Turn Water into Joy.

Pleasure Cove Marina is the launching point for houseboats on Lake Berryessa.

Distance from San Francisco to Lake Berryessa: *77 miles*
Drive time: *1 hour, 40 minutes*
Getting there: *US-101 S to I-80 E to I-505 N to CA-128 W*

1. PLEASURE COVE HOUSEBOAT RENTALS: 6100 Highway 128, Napa, CA 94558, +1 707.966.9600, www.goberryessa.com
Details: *Three boat sizes available, sleeping 10–12 people; $506–$1460 per night, depending on boat, season, and rental length.*

2. CLEMENTE'S AUTHENTIC ITALIAN TAKEOUT: 1531 Third Street, Napa, CA 94559, +1 707.224.2237, Facebook: Clemente's Italian Takeout

3. VEZÉR FAMILY WINERY: 2522 Mankas Corner Road, Fairfield, CA 94534, +1 707.429.3935, www.vezerfamilyvineyard.com

4. LAKE BERRYESSA BOAT & JET SKI RENTAL: 7521 Highway 128, Napa, CA 94558, +1 707.966.4204, www.lakeberryessaboats.com

5. HIGH WATER SUP: 100 Riverside Drive, Napa, CA 94558, +1 707.666.3388, www.highwatersup.com, highwatersup@gmail.com

6. FRATI GELATO: 670 Main Street, Napa, CA 94559, +1 707.265.0265, www.fratigelatocafe.com

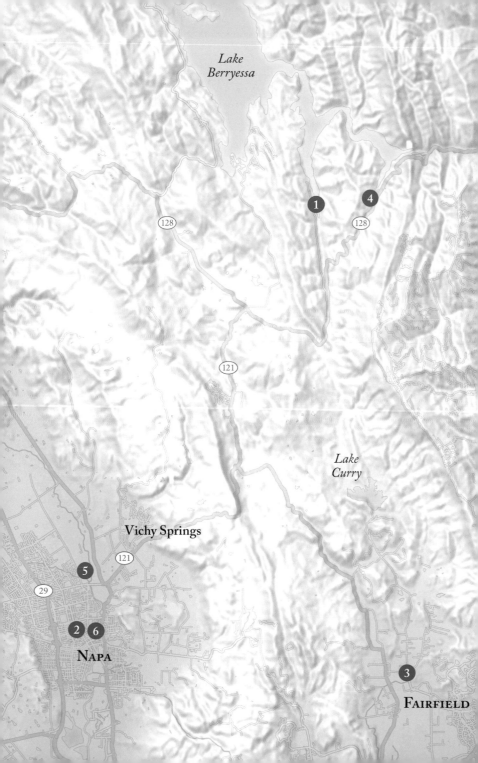

19

Surf City • *Half Moon Bay*

THE CHURCH OF SURF CONVENES IN HALF MOON BAY AND ITS cathedral is Mavericks – a surf break about a half mile offshore yielding massive waves that can reach as high as 60 feet. For those who surf here, it isn't a matter of *if* they are going to get pulled under but *when*, and this level of peril makes it a place for high holy days but not for daily prayer. Titans of Mavericks, perhaps the most famed annual surf competition in the world, is an invite-only big wave rush that brings together 24 of the sport's best surfers as well as enthusiasts from around the world who come to witness the daring spectacle. The scale and the danger of Mavericks have turned Half Moon Bay into a surfer's mecca.

Though Mavericks is now internationally known as the California beach with Hawaiian-sized waves, for a long time it was deeply local. So local, in fact, that only one guy rode it. Half Moon Bay native Jeff Clark had always thought the spot was too dangerous but in 1975, he decided to brave the waves. Clark pretty much had the place to himself until 1990, when a few friends joined him and a photo in *Surfer* magazine let the cat out of the bag.

The **Inn at Mavericks** is located in a surprisingly industrial neighborhood on the way to Mavericks Beach and it is also within walking distance of Pillar Point Harbor. Each of the six rooms has an ocean view and is named after a surfing beach. Check in, slip on your flip-flops and board shorts, and then stroll the few blocks to **Seville**, a vibrant little tapas restaurant with outdoor seating and a list of more than 40 small dishes to share and savor over sunset, like a *tortilla espanola*, with an accompanying glass of cava. For a nightcap at a classic surf hangout, duck in next door to the **Old Princeton Landing and Public House**. Manager Brian Overfelt is a surfer himself and the bar has long been a favorite coastal dive, even for hallowed local Neil Young, who played a rare show there in 1996.

If you haven't surfed, you should most definitely get a lesson. Dave Alexander is the man to see. He has been surfing the area since he was 12 years old and is fantastic with kids. In fact, he runs surf camps all summer for the wee ones. He also offers one-on-ones for surfers looking to improve their skill set. And if you want to bring your crew, you can arrange a group session. The surfboard comes with the lesson. You just need to bring a wet suit and an ability to swim.

Clockwise from top left: *Half Moon Bay vista; fashionable fins and boards at Mavericks Surf Shop; seaside fire pit at the Inn at Mavericks; Ketch Joanne's satisfying breakfast*

Mavericks Surf Shop can not only meet your wet-suit needs, they've also got all the surf-culture accessories to help you look the part – commemorative Titans T-shirts, beanies, Sex Wax, and skateboards. The super-approachable staff is knowledgeable about the local beaches, so they can act as concierges to the waves. Unless you're among the surfing elite, you won't be chancing life and limb at the often-treacherous Mavericks, but Dave is known for having a beat on the day's most righteous waves and is happy to advise.

When you bring your wet suit back to the surf shop, stop at **Ketch Joanne's**, a cozy diner for post-surf grub. Being on the water builds a ferocious hunger, and the food here is classic big-plate breakfast fare with a seaside touch, like cod in lieu of bacon with your eggs, toast, and hash browns. A wood-burning stove and just-big-enough booths add to the warmth of the atmosphere.

TIP: *After some nourishment, you might want to go back out on your own. Just consult the surf report to find your level of wave: www.surfline.com/surf-report/half-moon-bay-northern-california_5007.*

Freedom and improvisation kindle the spirits of surfing and jazz. **Bach Dancing & Dynamite Society** is a place to be consumed by both. Pete Douglas first opened his home to showcase serious jazz musicians in an intimate and reverential setting in 1964. Though Douglas passed away, his daughters have reopened the space to continue his vision. The concerts go from 4:30pm to 7pm and there are meals and snacks available, as well as a full bar, but you are welcome to bring a picnic, too. Dizzy Gillespie, Etta James, Count Basie, and Duke Ellington have all played this 160-seat nonprofit venue.

Tip: *Before the show, stop in downtown Half Moon Bay at* **Cowboy Fishing Co.***, which sticks to doing a few things really well – brewing beer and cooking crab.*

Downtown Half Moon Bay is off the water but still has salt in its gills. On Sunday morning, grab a breakfast pizza or fresh doughnut at **Half Moon Bay Bakery**, and then wander Main Street and check out all the shops. **Oddyssea** is a quirky favorite, both a store and a DIY-workshop. Buy handcrafted art, like an air plant and shell sculpture or make your own in a class or at home from their selection of beautiful objects.

On the way out of town, take a walk to **Mavericks** to pay homage. When you get to the parking lot, walk down the trail to the harbor and turn right. A radar station that looks like a giant white ball is a beacon from afar that will lead you to the beach. While high tide can be epic, low tide reveals hidden tide pools. Otters, gulls, and grebes are often sighted. Never turn your back on the ocean; never lose your sights on the sea.

A post-waves hoodie at Mavericks Surf Shop, which rents boards and wetsuits and sells gear.

Distance from San Francisco to Half Moon Bay: *30 miles*
Drive time: *45 minutes*
Getting there: *US-101 S to I-280 S to CA-92 W*

1. INN AT MAVERICKS: 346 Princeton Avenue, Half Moon Bay, CA 94019, +1 650.421.5300, www.innatmavericks.com
   Details: *Six rooms, each with ocean views, private balcony/patio, and snack service; $229–$406 per night. Pet friendly.*

2. SEVILLE TAPAS: 450 Capistrano Road, Half Moon Bay, CA 94019, +1 650.563.4181, www.sevilletapas.com

3. OLD PRINCETON LANDING: PUBLIC HOUSE AND GRILL: 460 Capistrano Road, El Granada, CA 94018, +1 650.728.7096, www.oplhmb.com

4. OPEN OCEAN SURFING: Surfer's Beach, Half Moon Bay, CA 94109, +1 650.867.0315, www.openoceansurfing.com, Facebook: Open Ocean Surf School

5. MAVERICKS SURF SHOP: 25 Johnson Pier, Half Moon Bay, CA 94019, +1 650.560.8088, www.maverickssurfshop.com

6. KETCH JOANNE'S RESTAURANT & HARBOR BAR: 17 Johnson Pier, Half Moon Bay, CA 94019, +1 650.728.3747, www.ketchjoanne.com

7. COWBOY FISHING CO: 730 Main Street, Half Moon Bay, CA 94019, +1 650.713.0811, www.cowboyfishing.com

8. BACH DANCING & DYNAMITE SOCIETY: 30711 Mirada Road, Half Moon Bay, CA 94019, +1 650.726.4143, www.bachddsoc.com

9. HALF MOON BAY BAKERY: 514 Main Street, Half Moon Bay, CA 94019, +1 650.726.4841

10. ODDYSSEA: 617 Main Street, Half Moon Bay, CA 94019, +1 650.440.4555, www.oddyssea.com

11. MAVERICKS BEACH: Pillar Point, Princeton-by-the-Sea, CA

El Granada

②
③
①
④
⑤
⑥
⑪
①

⑧

*Half Moon
Bay*

①

HALF MOON BAY

⑨
⑩
⑦

The beaches along the California coastline
have long been a surfer's paradise.

Camping Carnival • *Pescadero*

THE CARNIVAL COMMENCES BEFORE YOU EVEN HIT PESCADERO. THE last strip of Highway 92, before it dead-ends at Highway One, is like a perma-fair, switching focus through the seasons from pumpkins to Christmas trees to flowers but maintaining a country-circus buzz all year long, with hayrides, comedy shows, dinosaur statues, pony rides, and miles of greenhouses. The **Lemos Farm** is a particularly vibrant stop for kids, with outdoor laser tag and trains. The **Half Moon Bay Nurseries** comprise a strip mall of specialty plant outlets featuring succulents, carnivores, aquaponics, and native plants – one parking spot and your garden is planted. At Christmastime, the road slows to a festive crawl.

Costanoa is glamorous – i.e., camping here is a little more luxe than a backpacking trek. It makes for a gentle first step into sleeping under the stars, if you are nervous or low on equipment. And even for the avid outdoorsman, it is a well-maintained campground amid a bevy of natural environments worth exploring. If you stay in the lodge proper or the Douglas Fir Cabins, you are definitely more on the glam side of the scale, with fireplaces and mini-fridges. The tent bungalows, on the other hand, are further on the rugged end of the spectrum. The small white structures are basically already-erected tents with comfortable beds, arranged in a little village with outdoor grills and chairs, inviting cross-tent fraternization.

One of the pleasures of camping is setting up your site. Once you have unpacked, arranged, and unwound, take a good long walk. The grounds are completely surrounded by the wilderness of this "banana belt," a little pocket of land with warmer weather conditions than the surrounding area, allowing a diversity of flora and fauna to thrive. If you want to venture out for dinner, **Highway 1 Brewing Company** is down the road and specializes in comfort foods made from locally sourced ingredients and house-brewed beers, like "Pepper in the Rye," a rye beer with fresh-cracked peppercorns, and IPAs. On-site is the Cascade Bar & Grill, with more-upscale menu options, like diver scallops and grass-fed rib eye. They also have adventurous breakfast-menu items, such as Frosted Flake-crusted french toast and duck eggs with hash.

After breakfast and camp coffee, it's off to **Pie Ranch** – a triangle-shaped nonprofit farm on a mission, training the next generation of farmers and food activists. And they also make damn fine pie. The

CLOCKWISE FROM TOP LEFT: *Costanoa's Douglas Fir Cabins; Pigeon Point Lighthouse; tent bungalow interior at Costanoa; Año Nuevo State Beach; Pie Ranch spicy pickled carrots; plants for the curious along Highway 92*

twinkly-lit farm stand is a must stop, with pickled veggies, fresh-milled flour made from their own wheat, exotic varietals of dried chilies, and a library of books on food and sustainability. Get a bag of their pancake mix made from their Jammu wheat and a dozen big, orange-yolked duck eggs for Sunday breakfast. The pie is made in Santa Cruz from their own produce and the crust is flaky on the outside and densely buttery. Mini or regular-sized versions of Meyer lemon, chocolate, honey-and-nut, and other luscious flavors of pie keep company with savory galettes and shortbread cookies in the case. Take a self-guided tour of the farm after indulging at one of the picnic tables outside the barn.

Just down the road, **Año Nuevo State Beach** is a wide, flat sandy beach with lots of sun and wind that is custom-made to tire out kids and dogs or to fly a kite. If you plan to stay for a while, you might bring an umbrella. It is also home to the largest elephant seal rookery in the world. **Bean Hollow State Beach** is the next opportunity to touch the sea on your way north and is remarkable for its rich tide pools full of anemones, sea urchins, and their marine brethren.

After beachcombing, drive a few miles inland. There isn't much to tiny historic Pescadero, but that only makes it more of a super-concentrated beguilement. Start at **Downtown Local**, a third-wave coffee shop with a surprising retail section reflecting a curatorial zest for vintage and hipster goods – from ironic records (hello Jane Fonda workout soundtrack!) to beautifully illustrated tarot cards to all-natural skin-care products. In the back is a pocket movie theater rolling black-and-whites for any nine people who might be interested. Next door is the **Pescadero Country Store**, which has a fair selection of groceries but is also a legit pizzeria with a wood-burning oven. And if you need an afternoon snack, visit the overly named **Arcangeli Grocery Company/Norm's Market** for hot and divine artichoke-garlic herb bread, or stop in for a cold one and a bowl of cioppino at **Duarte's Tavern**, open since 1894.

Between Pie Ranch and the groceries in Pescadero, you should have ample material for a cabin feast. After dinner, meet some of your fellow glampers at the hot tub or the comfort station, which is where you will find bathroom amenities and, outside, a lovely stone fireplace with ample Adirondacks.

TIP: *Just 4.5 miles north of Costanoa off Highway One is **Pigeon Point Light Station**, the tallest lighthouse on the West Coast, at 115 feet. There is a rambling little path to the cliff edge, where you can view seals and whales when they are in the neighborhood.*

The route says one hour back to San Francisco, but you will likely find yourself tempted to pull over again and again – called off the road by lighthouses, laser tag, miles of yellow mustard flowers, and some of the most entrancing coastline in the world. Let your curiosity be your GPS.

Wild mustard dusts the fields in San Mateo County from January to March.

Distance from San Francisco to Pescadero: *47 miles*
Drive time: *1 hour*
Getting there: *CA-1 S to Pescadero Creek Rd*

1. Costanoa Lodge: 2001 Rossi Road, Pescadero, CA 94060, +1 650.879.1100, www.costanoa.com
Details: *Cabins, tents, or lodge rooms available; $95–$350 per night. All accommodations have either a private bath or bathroom access; linens provided. Restaurant and general store on-site.*

2. Lemos Farm: 12320 San Mateo Road, Half Moon Bay, CA 94019, +1 650.726.2342, www.lemosfarm.com

3. Half Moon Bay Nurseries: 11651–12511 San Mateo Road, Half Moon Bay, CA 94019, www.halfmoonbaynurseries.com

4. Highway 1 Brewing Company: 5720 Cabrillo Highway, Pescadero, CA 94060, +1 650.879.9243, www.highway1brewing.com

5. Pie Ranch: 2080 Cabrillo Highway, CA 94060, +1 650.879.0995, www.pieranch.org

6. Año Nuevo: Año Nuevo State Park Road, Pescadero, CA 94060, +1 650.879.2025, www.parks.ca.gov

7. Bean Hollow: New Years Creek Road, Pescadero, CA 94060, +1 650.726.8819, www.parks.ca.gov/?page_id=527

8. Downtown Local: 213 Stage Road, Pescadero, CA 94060, +1 650.879.9155, Facebook: Downtown Local

9. Pescadero Country Store: 251 Stage Road, Pescadero, CA 94060, +1 650.879.0410, www.pescaderocountrystore.com

10. Arcangeli Grocery Company/Norm's Market : 287 Stage Road, Pescadero, CA 94060, +1 650.879.0147, www.normsmarket.com

11. Duarte's Tavern: 202 Stage Road, Pescadero, CA 94060, +1 650.879.0464, www.duartestavern.com

12. Pigeon Point Light Station State Park: 210 Pigeon Point Road, Pescadero, CA 94060, +1 650.879.2120, www.parks.ca.gov

Silicon Slip Away • *San Jose & Palo Alto*

SILICON VALLEY HAS BECOME THE EPICENTER OF A PARADIGM SHIFT IN our evolution. This little collection of towns south of San Francisco has changed even the way we think and behave. And it all happens behind the walls of immense buildings scattered among colorful campuses just south of San Francisco. Oh, and sometimes in cafes. And sometimes in garages. Members of the tech industry travel in herds, and this weekend you will stalk some of the more interesting breeds.

Start in Palo Alto, much like Apple and Hewlett Packard did, though your trip will not likely involve sleepless nights. **Garden Court** is a boutique hotel with a modern, luxurious vibe that appeals to its venture-capitalist clientele. After you've checked in, scoot over to **Madera**, which boasts a notorious Silicon Valley bar scene. Observe the local VC set in their natural habitat over a martini and a Michelin-star meal, like Sonoma County Liberty duck with farro, young carrot, fennel, and satsuma mandarin.

Saturday morning is super civilized at **Mayfield Bakery & Cafe** in the Town & Country Village shopping center. Fabulous coffee and pastries are available to go or you can enjoy a Bloody Mary and kale florentine in the cafe, where the angel investors park their strollers. Just ten blocks away you'll find the **HP Garage**, often called the birthplace of Silicon Valley, where the famous duo built the audio oscillator that revolutionized the whole electronics industry.

A walk through the gracious neighborhood of "Professorville" will land you at Stanford, which turns out computer engineers from its atmosphere of stately oak-lined boulevards. The **Cantor Art Center** features ever-changing exhibitions that range widely, from the works of Edward Hopper to late-18th-century Asian costumes.

Time to get to the beating heart of the matter and move out of the investor quarters and into San Jose's tech sanctuary. The kings of computing are all notorious for keeping the ramparts high around their castles of innovation, but **Google** offers a peek inside its campus culture with their cartoonish statues. Take a selfie next to the anthropomorphized versions of their android operating system. The primary-hued bikes all around (hundreds of them), for employees only, have become ubiquitous icons of the valley. Apple, Facebook, and LinkedIn also have campus wheels but none quite so visible as Google.

CLOCKWISE FROM TOP LEFT: *HP's origin story begins in this garage; imposing beauty at Stanford University; kids get involved at The Tech; San Pedro Square Market Bar; buttery, curried garbanzos and fish at Mayfield Cafe & Bakery* OPPOSITE: *Play with pricey tech toys at TechShop in San Jose.*

TIP: *For a real insider commute to your vacation, bike from San Francisco, like the SF2G (San Francisco to Google) Riding Club. Check out www.sf2g.com for routes and club rides.*

Downtown San Jose provides some opportunities to get inside the bubble and not just peek at it from the outside. **The Tech Museum of Innovation**, especially enthralling for kids, connects visitors with all kinds of modern inventions and tools – you can play with robotics, design your own virtual roller coaster, and witness how tech solves medical issues in the operating room and beyond. Have an afternoon snack around the corner at the hip indoor food court, **San Pedro Square Market Bar**, offering a cornucopia of culinary choices, from ice cream to sushi. Saturday night is time for a DIYer date at **TechShop San Jose**, a club that allows members to use awesome equipment – like 3D printers – without having to buy it themselves. Check their calendar for their MITI (Make It, Take It) couples classes that don't require membership, such as laser etching of wineglasses.

Every creative knows you also need to disconnect to be truly connected. Now that you've fully steeped your mind in the cerebral tea of the Valley, it's time to wring it out. Head to the darling Silicon exurb of Saratoga and find an outdoor table at the wildly popular **Bella Saratoga** for a mimosa and eggs Benedict. Just outside of town is **Castle Rock State Park**, serving up stunning views without a think tank in sight. The trailhead starts at the ridgeline of the Santa Cruz Mountains and looks down into the wild forest of redwoods, Douglas firs, and madrones. Unique rock formations make the park popular with climbers.

Continue your homeward trajectory north to **Aruna Spa,**[1] in Mountain View. The owner discovered a sea-salt-water floating pool in London, and was so enamored she decided to bring the experience to America. Unlike the total sensory deprivation of most float tanks, this one pulls you gently away from the super-stimulation of Silicon Valley in a quiet meditative room. The pool can be shared with your weekend companion(s) and provides a sense of utter buoyancy, taking the weight of the world off of your fingertips.

Distance from San Francisco to San Jose: *48 miles*
Drive time: *1 hour*
Getting there: *US-101 S to CA-87 S*

1. GARDEN COURT HOTEL: 520 Cowper Street, Palo Alto, CA 94301, +1 650.322.9000, www.gardencourt.com
   Details: *62 rooms with options for a spa tub, fireplace, and other amenities; $299–$549 per night.*

2. MADERA: 2825 Sand Hill Road, Menlo Park, CA 94025, +1 650.561.1540, www.madersandhill.com

3. MAYFIELD CAFÉ & BAKERY: 855 El Camino Real, Palo Alto, CA 94301, +1 650.853.9200, www.mayfield.com

4. HP GARAGE: 369 Addison Avenue, Palo Alto, CA, 94301

5. CANTOR ARTS CENTER AT STANFORD UNIVERSITY: 328 Lomita Drive, Stanford, CA 94305, +1 650.723.4177, www.museum.stanford.edu

6. GOOGLE ANDROID STATUES: 1981 Landings Drive, Mountain View, CA 94043

7. THE TECH MUSEUM OF INNOVATION: 291 South Market Street, San Jose, CA 95113, +1 408.294.8324, www.thetech.com

8. SAN PEDRO SQUARE MARKET BAR: 87 North San Pedro Street, San Jose, CA 95110, +1 408.444.7227, www.sanpedrosquaremarket.com

9. TECHSHOP SAN JOSE: 300 South Second Street, San Jose, CA 95113, +1 408.916.4144, www.techshop.ws

10. BELLA SARATOGA: 14503 Big Basin Way, Saratoga, CA 95070, +1 408.741.5115, www.bellasaratoga.com

11. CASTLE ROCK STATE PARK: 15000 Skyline Boulevard, CA 95033, +1 408.867.2952, www.parks.ca.gov/?page_id=538

12. ARUNA SPA: 2500 California Street, Mountain View, CA 94040, +1 650.949.1800, www.arunadayspa.com

Hard to believe Silicon Valley is just a few miles from this awesomely low-tech view.

Brewhaha · *Petaluma & Santa Rosa*

BEER, LIKE WINE BEFORE IT (AND COFFEE AND CIDER) IS IN ITS "third wave" of discovery. The first wave was the Old World origins, which consisted of monks creating the first ales and lasted until the Industrial Age. Then came the second wave's mass production, which allowed beers to travel to every inch of the globe, albeit in often watered-down, inauthentic versions. The recent renaissance of the craft of brewing, which has introduced time-honored traditions to the present moment with fresh takes on technique and ingredients, constitutes the third wave. Though Sonoma County is wine country, it is also decidedly beer country. A few early masters of the craft-beer revolution can be found in Santa Rosa, and newcomers are flocking to what is becoming a true beer district in Petaluma. Are these breweries riding the third-wave peak or do they represent the dawn of yet a fourth wave? Let us surf the suds.

> TIP: *Depending on your hour of departure, 101 North can be a drag, especially on a Friday afternoon. If you need to escape the slow jam, stop in San Rafael at Sol Food's original location, AKA Small Space at 811 Fourth Street. This little kiosk of excellent Puerto Rican fare is close to the freeway but feels like a vacation. Sip on an Arnoldo Palmero (half mango iced tea, half limeade) and let the unimaginative fume in traffic.*

There are many a fancy accommodation option in Sonoma County, but few with the personality of **Metro Hotel**, on Petaluma's south side. Its Parisian flea market quirkiness is balanced with sumptuous bedding and fresh crepes for breakfast. For a truly private and kitschy sleep experience, request one of the two fitted-out Airstreams, with cuddly bed nooks and kitchenettes as well as Astroturf front yards. *Sunset* magazine designated Metro as one of the top 20 unique hotels in the west.

Taps is the first stop on your craft-beer crawl. Aptly named for its wall of beer taps, here you can get the lay of the brewscape and suss out local options. Northern California is mad for hops, and you will find lots of IPAs on offer. But there are deeper cuts available too. A menu of snacks is custom-built to prolong your drinking capacity, including

perfectly caramelized brussels sprouts and juicy hot dogs. Nab a spot near the picture windows or outside on the convivial deck to enjoy one of the best views in town of the Petaluma River, flowing by like so much pilsner.

After a good night of rest on a scrumptious down-topped bed, it's time for a more pointed intake of beer. Best to get your suds with a bit of education, to slow the effect, if nothing else. Head to the beer district (not officially known as such yet, but considered to be by the cognoscenti), an industrial area that is populated by excellent craft breweries, including the national favorite and forever cheeky **Lagunitas**. No longer the little guy, but not a big guy, either, Lagunitas has daily tours and merch for miles. But if you have never been, paying homage to one of the original trailblazers of the third wave is a must. With a sassy brand personality (beer names like the Hairy Eyeball, meant to stop a hangover at the first achy blink), quality product, and a generous policy for sponsoring all kinds of events, Lagunitas has grown into a healthy company that has given Americans a taste for those hop-heavy NorCal beers.

Start your day with the informal formality of a Lagunitas tour (every hour, on the hour from 1pm to 5pm on weekends). Sort of like a (free!) awesome, alcoholic traffic school, it starts off in a cozy lounge that feels like your older brother's room in high school, with posters on every flat surface. While you polish off four taster-size glasses of beer, a bartender/docent shares the history of Lagunitas with a great deal of humor, after which you visit the brewery floor.

Now that you have your bearings, or beerings, and your buzz is probably wearing off, it's time to trot right off the beaten path. Luckily we aren't going far, so you can walk across the street to the next stop: **Petaluma Hills Brewing Company**. Owner and brewmaster JJ Jay (yep), has a different, and less hoptastic, approach to beer making. His ambitious repertoire, from pilsners to porters, is based on a passion for producing the best possible version of a traditional brew. In a landscape of fruity ales and over-the-top imperials ("Imperial" tacked on to a beer name means it is higher in alcohol and often has a more intense flavor, sometimes achieved with a great deal of hops), Jay seeks a subtler purity. While most breweries start to consolidate to just a few yeasts and flavors to increase profit, Jay is keeping his mad laboratory diverse in order to create create faithful iterations with his own touch.

The taproom has the atmosphere of a casual den and offers an unfiltered view of the tanks. If Jay is around, he might even give you a personal tour. Current laws don't allow a kitchen on-site, but they have a catalogue of pretzel snacks and a dart board and you are encouraged to bring your own eats or call for delivery right to the taproom (Old Chicago Pizza is a Petaluma institution and their deep-dish pies will sustain you through a flight: +1 707.766.8600 or www.oldchgo.com). You can order bombers (22 ounces), growlers (64 ounces), or a keg of

CLOCKWISE FROM TOP LEFT: *Petaluma's Metro Hotel; tasters at Petaluma Hills Brewing; Taps' brussels sprouts; Petaluma Hills owner, J.J. Jay, in his element*

ABOVE: *Woodfour's wall of beer at the Barlow*
BELOW: *Toasting at Taps in Petaluma*

your favorite brew to go. Curate your own tasting flight for a generous and reasonable tipple. You can hear some good Petaluma stories by asking about the origin of the beer names, each of which is linked to a local legend or landmark.

While the other breweries in the area are not open to the public, there is a craft distiller right down the block. **Griffo Distillery** makes a whiskey and a London style gin. Happy to show you around, with prior reservations, they are focused on the kind of terroir and craft that makes them part of third-wave liquor, a more boutique, newer movement than that of beer, coffee, or wine. For an even more special visit, sign up on their website to be put on the list for their bottling parties. When your name comes up, you'll be invited to help get the booze out the door and paid for your labor with food, music, and, of course, a little handcrafted hooch.

TIP: *If you want to add another stop to your ale-ducation, pull into the Barlow in Sebastopol on your beer crawl north to Santa Rosa. The center has many nice wine (gasp!) tasting rooms and shops, but most important, it's home to* **Woodfour Brewing Co.***, which brews an eclectic array of beers.*

Unless you stowed a sandwich in your pocket, you are surely ready for dinner. Get your designated driver (or Uber chauffeur) to take you to Santa Rosa's **Toad in the Hole**, a gastropub in Railroad Square, a sweet quarter of the county seat. The Toad has above-the-norm pub fare without a trying-too-hard vibe. The burger is excellent and the Ploughman's Plate, which is sort of like an English pupu platter, is hearty and nourishing. As with many pubs in the area, the beer selection is thoughtful, and they also always have a keg of "real ale," or cask ale, which is beer that is made from traditional ingredients and continues to ferment in the cask from which it is served, so it is enzymatically alive and more complex than the usual tap or bottled beer. Order from the cask for a unique and "ancient" experience, harkening back to a time when beer, with its fervid mineral activity, was part of the nutritional makeup of a meal.

After a bite and a half pint of real ale, the quest continues. Get some fresh air while walking from Railroad Square to Fourth Street's **Russian River Brewing Company** – a consistent award winner at the Great American Beer Festival and World Beer Cup. Russian River is a perfect place for a flight because they offer a ton of beer options, many of them only seasonally available. At this point, your taste buds have been through the wringer, so you will appreciate the big flavors of their hopped-up style. As with any flight, start with lighter pilsners and move up to more robust ales, ending with dark porter and stout styles.

Ready to call it a night? Head back to your Airstream and dream of toasty hops and waves of wheat, in the magical place where tradition and terroir come crashing into a third wave of intoxication.

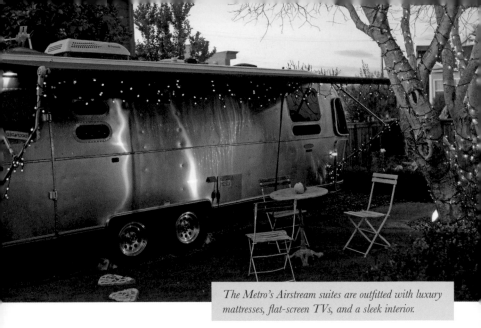

The Metro's Airstream suites are outfitted with luxury mattresses, flat-screen TVs, and a sleek interior.

Distance from San Francisco to Petaluma: *40 miles*
Drive time: *50 minutes*
Getting there: *US-101 N to Petaluma Blvd S*

1. METRO HOTEL: 508 Petaluma Boulevard South, Petaluma, CA 94952, +1 707.773.4900, www.metrolodging.com
   Details: *Each room has an individual vibe; $120–$250 per night.*

2. TAPS BEER CO. & KITCHEN: 54 East Washington Street, Petaluma, CA 94952, +1 707.763.6700, www.petalumataps.com

3. LAGUNITAS BREWING COMPANY: 1280 North McDowell Boulevard, Petaluma, CA 94954, +1 707.769.4495, www.lagunitas.com

4. PETALUMA HILLS BREWING COMPANY: 1333 North McDowell Boulevard, Suite A, Petaluma, CA 94954, +1 707.766.4458, www.petalumahills.com

5. GRIFFO DISTILLERY: 1320 Scott Street, Suite A, Petaluma, CA 94954, +1 707.879.8755, www.griffodistillery.com

6. WOODFOUR BREWING COMPANY: 6780 Depot Street, Sebastopol, CA 95472, +1 707.824.3144, www.woodfourbrewing.com

7. THE TOAD IN THE HOLE: 116 Fifth Street, Santa Rosa, CA 95401, +1 707.544.TOAD (8623), www.thetoadpub.com

8. RUSSIAN RIVER BREWING COMPANY: 725 Fourth Street, Santa Rosa, CA 95404, +1 707.545.BEER (2337), www.russianriverbrewing.com

23

Agri-cultured • *Petaluma, Sebastopol & Santa Rosa*

In other parts of the country, farming is a living. In Sonoma County it is a lifestyle. And not because farmers in this diverse county don't work as hard or as earnestly as in other rural areas, but because farming is so admired here – so bathed in laurel – that it is chic to be "farmy."

Nothing could draw you into the romance of Sonoma's farm culture more than the bespoke agrarianism of **Weber Ranch** in Petaluma – your home away from home for the weekend. Owned by the same family that's behind Della Fattoria, one of the most respected bakeries in Northern California, the farm is host to one-of-a-kind events, the bread-making side of their operation, and a few guest lodgings. The smell of baking levains and baguettes alone is worth the trip. Comfy and squared away, you can rent what amounts to an apartment here for the night and then wake up to find your kitchen stocked with all the ingredients for a farmstead breakfast. Farmstead means everything is made where it is grown and in this instance, it also means that it is eaten where it is made. Fresh bread, fresh butter, fresh eggs.

> Tip: *The rolling hills along the western edge of Petaluma are home to the exquisite* **McEvoy Ranch** *– an example of glam agrarian at its finest. You need an appointment to experience the 550-acre ranch outside of workshop and tour days, so check the calendar on their website for upcoming events, and plan ahead. Visit for a wine or olive-oil tasting or a tour of their stunning grounds, including 80 acres of organic olive trees and 7 acres of grapevines.*

Once nourished and dowsed in the deep sleep that accompanies true quiet, head north to Santa Rosa and find the **Luther Burbank Home and Gardens** in downtown. Around the turn of the last century, Luther Burbank was an internationally renowned botanist, famous for his contributions to agriculture. All told, he created more than 800 varieties of living things, even a potato that helped to reverse the Irish potato famine. And the rampant experimentation that led to his many discoveries happened at his home (and on a nearby 15-acre farm). Lovely docents and signage make this a short, sweet tour that is long on historical perspective. Burbank brought us the Shasta daisy, spineless cactus, Santa Rosa plum and other plants.

After you have wandered the quaint grounds and meandered through his greenhouse (mysteriously, this glass building was one of the rare structures to survive the 1906 earthquake), you can follow in Burbank's footsteps to his farm in Sebastopol, where he housed his most experimental projects, and where his work still grows and is tended. Burbank rode his bike the 12 miles between the two properties regularly, always dressed in a suit and hat. By car it is a mere 15-minute drive. The small agricultural plot feels oddly located, amid a condominium complex that has grown up around it. There isn't much in the way of signage or explication, but the walk is a pleasant loop, especially near sunset, full of esoteric trees and plants.

TIP: *On your way from Santa Rosa to Sebastopol, take a detour off of Highway 12 on Llano Road to* **Joe Matos Cheese Co.** *Bring cash to get a chunk of St. George, a true farmstead cheese, as well as the heady inhale of a working dairy.*

Once in Sebastopol, you must visit the Barlow, a newish shopping center reanimating a previously cantankerous-looking warehouse district in the tiny town. Hotly designed and built up, the center hosts many wine-tasting opportunities and some good shopping. **Zazu Kitchen + Farm** will be easy to find – just look for the giant tin pig head hanging outside. Chefs (and spouses) John Stewart and Duskie Estes make their menus from the most ripe and ready produce sourced on their own farm and from local purveyors whom they love. Zazu is also known for its salumi and they make their own bacon under the label Black Pig Bacon Co., which is worth hunting down.

Tip: *For a place to purchase Black Pig Bacon Co.'s dynamite pork belly, visit www.blackpigmeatco.com/find-bacon/*

On the drive back to your repose is a restaurant called **Peter Lowell's**, on the westernmost tip of Sebastopol. The bar there is open until 10pm

A Sonoma County farm, next door to Joe Matos Cheese Co., complete with vintage John Deeres.

CLOCKWISE FROM TOP LEFT: *Della Fattoria's luscious chocolate pot de crème; the greenhouse at Luther Burbank's home in Santa Rosa; Petaluma's Thistle Meats specializes in whole-animal butchery; Weber Ranch residents; accommodations at Weber Ranch; Petaluma Seed Bank is housed in an elegant former bank*

and they have a nice list of biodynamic, organic local wines (whatever adjective suits your fancy). Have a nightcap and toast the farmers in your life.

Day Two begins with the blessing of breaking bread, again, and beautiful bread it is. After walking the grounds of the ranch, replete with animalia, including sheep, goats and a gregarious herd of dogs, Petaluma awaits. Downtown Petaluma is a farm town that is slowly becoming more full of concentrated charm. Grab a coffee at **Acre**, which roasts its own beans locally. The shop's interior is outfitted with reclaimed lumber from an old warehouse. Take your double-shot cappuccino along with you and let the metaphorical dirt cake your boots.

Head first to **Thistle Meats**, a butcher shop that buys its meat directly from local farms and only purchases the whole animal. This means it is a "real" butcher shop, offering a variety of cuts that many of us are unaccustomed to seeing in the grocery store's meat department. On a weekend away, you may not be up for heavy-duty food shopping (although you can cook at Weber Ranch), but you must not leave Thistle without some house-made charcuterie – dense patés, spicy salami, rustic mortadella. They also offer a hearty sandwich of the day, and on Saturdays, you can get a truly special burger from their ad hoc grill set up in the alley behind the shop.

Several other boutiques are worth a wander – check out **Maude** for hipster household and gardening goods and clothing for women and children – embroidered baby smocks, artisan brooms, mushroom knives, chunky sweaters in saturated hues – or browse **Sienna**, a 14,000-square-foot antiques emporium that boasts treasures ranging from mid-century modern furnishings to 19th-century objects.

> TIP: Petaluma's **Green String Farm**, a longtime producer for Chez Panisse and other locally sourcing restaurants, can be experienced in a few ways: swing by for their monthly tour, the first Saturday at noon (weather permitting); arrange a private tour by emailing farmtours@greenstringfarm.com; or just visit their farm store and fill your sack with whatever is in season.

Make your next stop in town at the **Seed Bank**, which is closed on Saturdays – a garden shop in an historic bank building, with grand ceilings and stately marble floors. An inspiring collection of heirloom varietals, how-to books, tools, and farming products is quaintly juxtaposed to the elegant surroundings. The staff is friendly and knowledgeable and even if you aren't a farmer, you may leave with some ambitious plans for your backyard or picture window.

Pop into **Della Fattoria's** for a road snack (try a Fat Ho – their over-stuffed take on the Ho Ho) and pick up a loaf of bread (the local favorite is the rosemary–Meyer lemon) to take home with you. Flourishing and flush, head back to whatever jungle awaits you.

Springtime blossoms on Green String Farm in Petaluma precede summertime fruit.

Distance from San Francisco to Petaluma: *40 miles*
Drive time: *50 minutes*
Getting there: *US-101 N to Petaluma Blvd S*

1. WEBER RANCH: Contact via VRBO at: www.vrbo.com/348361/ or +1 707.529.2701
Details: *Two cottages available, each sleeps two; averages $129 per night.*

2. McEvoy RANCH: 5935 Red Hill Road, Petaluma, CA 94952, +1 707.769.4138, www.mcevoyranch.com, visit@mcevoyranch.com

3. LUTHER BURBANK HOME & GARDENS: 204 Santa Rosa Avenue, Santa Rosa, CA 95404, +1 707.524.5445, www.lutherburbank.org

4. LUTHER BURBANK EXPERIMENT FARM: 7781 Bodega Avenue, Sebastopol, CA 95472, +1 707.829.6711

5. ZAZU KITCHEN + FARM: 6770 McKinley Street #150, Sebastopol, CA 95472, +1 707.523.4814, www.zazukitchen.com

6. PETER LOWELL'S: 7385 Healdsburg Avenue #101, Sebastopol, CA 95472, +1 707.829.1077, www.peterlowells.com

7. JOE MATOS CHEESE CO.: 3669 Llano Road, Santa Rosa, CA 95407, +1 707.584.5283

8. ACRE COFFEE: 21 Fourth Street, Petaluma, CA 94952, +1 707.772.5117, www.acrecoffee.com

9. THISTLE MEATS: 160 Petaluma Boulevard North, Petaluma, CA 94952, +1 707.772.5442, www.thistlemeats.com

10. MAUDE: 10 Western Avenue, Petaluma, CA 94952, +1 707.763.1858, www.maudeshop.com

11. SIENNA ANTIQUES: 119 Petaluma Boulevard North, Petaluma, CA 94952, +1 707.763.6088, www.siennaantiques.com

12. GREEN STRING FARM: 3571 Old Adobe Rd, Petaluma, CA 94954, +1 707.778.7500, www.greenstringfarm.com

13. PETALUMA SEED BANK: 199 Petaluma Boulevard North, Petaluma, CA 94952, +1 707.773.1336, Facebook: Petaluma Seed Bank

14. DELLA FATTORIA: 141 Petaluma Boulevard North, Petaluma, CA 94952, +1 707.763.0161, www.dellafattoria.com

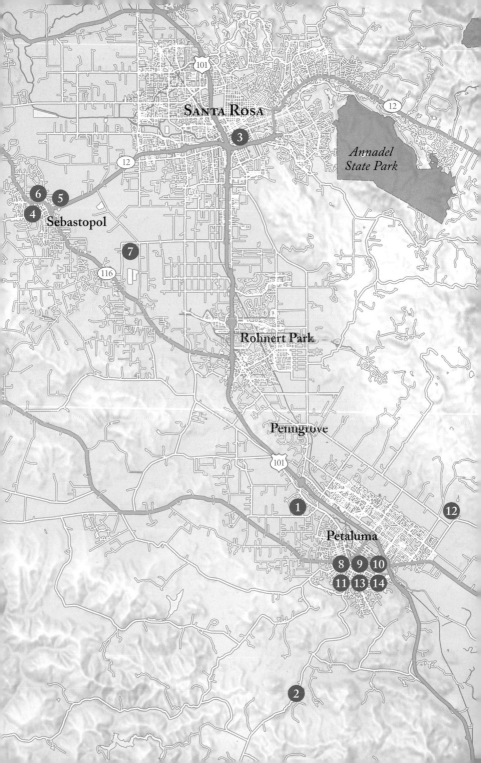

24

Alta California · *Sonoma*

THOUGH THE CITIES OF VALLEJO AND BENICIA WERE POSTHUMOUSLY named for General Vallejo and his wife, respectively, the town of Sonoma was their longtime home. Mariano Guadalupe Vallejo was deeply tied up in the formation of the State of California – or Alta California, as it is known in Mexico – and it all went down here. The layers of the past show through in the centuries-old buildings that are scattered around the central square and on the outskirts of downtown – making the history of Mexico and California's complicated relationship viscerally present.

The **El Dorado Hotel** is in one of the old western-expansion buildings along the perimeter of the square, but the rooms are modern and full of light, with garden patios on the ground floor and balconies upstairs. The hotel's restaurant, El Dorado Kitchen, or Ed K, as it is known, is not only a convenient place to begin your weekend, but also a delicious one. Drop your bags, head downstairs to the heated saltwater swimming pool, and then install yourself in the Ed K lounge area for a martini and truffle fries.

> TIP: *For breakfast, Ed K's makes nontraditional huevos rancheros, using flatbread instead of tortillas. Rancho Gordo beans and chorizo intensify the flavor.*

Just east of the hotel on the square is the **Sonoma Barracks,** a humble two-story adobe that originally housed Mexican soldiers sent to control Native-American resistance and was the site of the Bear Flag Revolt of 1846, so called because a group of Americans, wanting to take the territory from Mexico, defiantly flew the flag of the California Republic there. That uprising ended when the U.S. Navy arrived a month later, raising the U.S. flag in front of the barracks. The Mexican-American War was only two months old and had just landed in California, which remained a military-occupied enemy territory until September 9, 1850, when it finally achieved statehood.

Also on the square is **Mission San Francisco Solano,** the last mission built by the Mexicans, and the one farthest north. Its purpose was to keep Russian settlers in Bodega Bay and Fort Ross from gaining too much inland traction. A short half-mile walk through the Montini Open Space Reserve takes you to Vallejo's home for more than 35 years,

CLOCKWISE FROM TOP LEFT: *Housemade tortilla chips from El Molino Central; road sign for Ceja Vineyards' tasting room; Swiss Chalet at Lachrya Montis; Sonoma Barracks; Sonoma Plaza's Bear Flag Monument; servant's quarters at "Casa Grande," General Vellejo's first adobe home*

where he moved after he helped convince Mexico to cede California to the Americans and after he became a state senator. He named the estate **Lachryma Montis** ("mountain tear"), a rough Latin adaptation of the Native-American name Chicuyem ("crying mountain"), after an abundant spring on the property, which, for many years, provided water to the town of Sonoma and ultimately became the source of the reservoir you can visit today. The koi there are thought to be descendants of the very first carp introduced to the U.S. in the 1870s. The house is staged to look like the Vallejo family would have had it. At the top of the property is a little one-room cabin where Vallejo's son Napoleon kept a domestic zoo of as many as 14 dogs, a parrot, and numerous cats.

A walk back to the square will ring your inner lunch bell. **Tortilleria Jalisco** makes excellent tacos. Dollar tacos (that actually cost $2), street tacos, tacos de plaza – whatever you like to call them – come with two small corn tortillas, a pile of meat of your choosing, onion, and cilantro, in ascending order. Their hot sauce is no joke, but try not to blow out your taste buds before the next stop.

Ceja Vineyards is owned by the first-generation Mexican-American winemaking Ceja family, and their $20 tasting flight introduces you to their Carneros-region wines in a laid-back, elegant setting. Winemaker Armando Ceja and his sister-in-law Amelia were raised by Mexican immigrants who worked the vines for others, and now their family produces critically respected wines of their own. A few miles west, you will find another acclaimed Latino vineyard, **Robledo Family Winery**, where you can sample six of viticulturist Reynaldo Robledo's wines. He came to the United States in 1968 and spent 30 years employed by wineries and building his knowledge about every aspect of winemaking, from pruning to management, before he opened his winery in 2003, the first owned by a former migrant worker in California.

TIP: *Check the MAVA (Mexican-American Vintners Association) website to find more Latino-owned wineries in the Napa and Sonoma regions: www.nsmava.org.*

Continue to embrace the weekend's theme with dinner in Boyes Hot Springs, a small residential area with a largely Latino population and a high concentration of taquerias. One stands far above the rest: **El Molino Central** is colorful and bustling, with only outdoor seating. Everything is prepared in-house, including the corn tortillas made with hand-ground corn, giving them a toothsome complexity. This is a true rarity (nearly all corn tortillas are made from Maseca, a brand of instant corn flour). This fresh masa (dough) makes their tamales a must-order.

Sunday mornings in the plaza are slow and sunny. Have a freshly baked croissant at **Basque Boulangerie Café**, shop the artfully curated fair-trade goods at **Global Heart**, or pick up some aged Vella Jack cheese at **Sonoma Creamery**, which has been on the square since 1931.

For lunch, dig into the California-Mayan cuisine at **Maya**. Or nosh pepitas and sip a margarita at the bar. You can order a half shot of any of their more than 100 tequilas.

Sonoma echoes the stories of Russians, Native Americans, Spaniards, Mexicans, Americans from the east, and others, all discovering and imprinting the area with their own cultures. The tales are passed on now in the ever-evolving historic plaza and the communities surrounding it.

Distance from San Francisco to Sonoma: *45 miles*
Drive time: *1 hours*
Getting there: *US-101 N to CA-37 E to CA-121 N*

1. EL DORADO HOTEL & KITCHEN: 405 First Street West, Sonoma, CA 95476, +1 707.996.3030, www.eldoradosonoma.com
Details: *Rooms overlook Sonoma Plaza, the hotel courtyard, or pool; $275–$395 per night. Book in advance and note that weekends require a two-night minimum.*

2. SONOMA BARRACKS: 20 East Spain Street, Sonoma, CA 95476, +1 707.935.6832, www.sonomaparks.org

3. MISSION SAN FRANCISCO SOLANO: 114 East Spain Street, Sonoma, CA 95476, +1 707.938.9560, www.sonomaparks.org

4. LACHRYMA MONTIS: Third Street West, Sonoma, CA 95476, +1 707.938.9559, www.sonomaparks.org

5. TORTILLERIA JALISCO: 897 West Napa Street, Sonoma, CA 95476, +1 707.935.7356

6. CEJA VINEYARDS SONOMA WINE TASTING ROOM: 22989 Burndale Road, Sonoma, CA 95476, +1 707.931.6978, www.cejavineyards.com

7. ROBLEDO FAMILY WINERY: 21901 Bonness Road, Sonoma, CA 95476, +1 707.939.6903, www.robledofamilywinery.com

8. EL MOLINO CENTRAL: 11 Central Avenue, Sonoma, CA 95476, +1 707.939.1010, www.elmolinocentral.com

9. BASQUE BOULANGERIE CAFÉ: 490 First Street East, Sonoma, CA 95476, +1 707.935.7687, www.basqueboulangerie.com

10. GLOBAL HEART FAIR TRADE: 423 First Street West, Sonoma, CA 95476, +1 707.939.2847, www.globalheartfairtrade.blogspot.com

11. SONOMA CREAMERY: 670 West Napa Street, Sonoma, CA 95476, +1 707.996.1000, www.sonomacreamery.com

12. MAYA RESTAURANT: 101 East Napa Street, Sonoma, CA 95476, +1 707.935.3500, www.mayarestaurant.com

California state flags hang everywhere on Sonoma Plaza, where the first bear flag was raised in 1846.

The Pleasure Class · *Sonoma & Glen Ellen*

You can't wait for inspiration. You have to go after it with a club.

– Jack London

LET'S IMAGINE FOR A MOMENT LONDON MEANT A GOLF CLUB, AS THE course near his Sonoma County home is one of the country's finest. No one wore pleasure better than Jack London, the novelist laureate of Glen Ellen, and his wife, Charmian. From their estate in Glen Ellen, Beauty Ranch, they entertained, traveled, and followed their passions with gusto. Not born wealthy, London was one of the first American writers to achieve affluence and fame for his literary contributions in his own lifetime. Even now, 100 years after his death, his name and face are etched into the Northern California landscape. The aspect of his legacy we explore this weekend is not his socialism, his atheism, or his alcoholism but his *joie de vivre* and the institutions of fine living in Sonoma.

In the next town over, the **Fairmont Sonoma Mission Inn & Spa** is ready-made to maximize the pleasure principle. The Boyes hot springs that bubble up here have been a commercial endeavor since T. M. Leavenworth raised a hotel above them in 1845. London adored soaking in the steamy, mineral-rich springs and so shall you.

But, first, *joie* begins with a meal. **Café La Haye** is not as old as Sonoma Mission Inn but it is a local dining institution, nonetheless. Superb ingredients and preparation of wine-country cuisine matched with a tiny kitchen and only 32 seats make a reservation hard to come by. Book in advance to enjoy stellar execution of classic dishes like a buttermilk-brined pork chop with chorizo butter.

Another classic Sonoma restaurant is the **Big 3**, now part of the Fairmont property and open for 50 years. An upscale diner, it's the place to fill up for a day on the links or at the spa. Known for their lemon-and-cottage cheese pancakes, their menu hits every breakfast note from a selection of pastries to Dungeness crab benedict.

One of the jewels in the Fairmont Sonoma Mission Inn & Spa crown is **Sonoma Golf Club**. The course offers 360-degree views of the surrounding vineyards and the Mayacamas Mountains. The culmination of the PGA Champions Tour, this challenging 18-hole course was built in the 1920s, the golden age of golf architecture. Many par threes and two par fives will make this an afternoon of pitched pleasure. Al Barkow

CLOCKWISE FROM TOP LEFT: *Aetna Springs golf course; greens and traps at Sonoma Golf Club; Watsu pool at Fairmont Sonoma Mission Inn & Spa; the House of Happy Walls in Jack London State Park; Scupltures ite installation by Ivan McLean in Glen Ellen*
OPPOSITE: *Jack and Charmian London in mural form on the hike to Jack's gravesite.*

of *Links* magazine said, "As with a classic novel, each encounter reveals a nuance missed the last time around." You now must be a member or a guest of the hotel to play the course, and luckily, you are.

> TIP: *If you prefer something more off the beaten path, try shooting up to **Aetna Springs**. A former famous healing resort, its scenic 9-hole public course now stands alone and often has openings on Saturdays (they are closed Sundays). The luxurious clubhouse has a bocce court and a gorgeous and comfortable setting for picnics.*

After hours of outdoor exertion, head back to the hotel and take to the waters. A bathing ceremony is an ancient rite and one that any pleasure-seeker enjoys. Though the spa now offers many treatments, the facilities themselves are treatment enough. Soak in the hot mineral springs, then move to the body-temperature Watsu pool, and float right into dinner.

Around for nearly 20 years (that's 100 in restaurant years), **LaSalette** serves sumptuous Portugese food, emigrated and innovated. You'll find traditional dishes like caldo verde (potato soup with beef stock) but there are also truffle fries, because a New York steak needs truffle fries.

Sunday morning, call the front desk and order a yoga mat, MP3 player, and some Reebok apparel for a quiet workout in your room. After down dogs and sit-ups, breakfast is served at **Fig Café** in Glen Ellen, owned by east Sonoma County restaurateur Sondra Bernstein. Start with a "Fig Royale," a play on the Kir Royale, with fig aperitif taking the place of framboise. Indulge in the Francophile menu with a croque madame or omelet du jour.

After breakfast, visit Beauty Ranch, in **Jack London State Historic Park**, which is still a working testament to London's vertiginous creativity. The estate paints a very clear image of a marriage of two deeply individual but connected people. They each had their own sanctuary – hers a light-filled bedroom and his a tiny alcove adjacent to his office where he took catnaps while writing. A clothesline on which he clipped notes still hangs. Tour the farm with a docent to hear about London's successful farming

breakthroughs (an innovative pigsty, or piggery, that still stands) and his failures (his rabid promotion of eucalyptus trees was in part responsible for their invasive outgrowth). A hike through the park will take you not only to the site of the couple's ranch and unrealized dream home (the Wolf House – named after London's novel *The Sea-Wolf* – which burned to the ground a few weeks before they planned to move in), but also to Jack's grave and Charmian's home after London's death – the House of Happy Walls, as Charmian called it – which today is a museum displaying relics of their many sailing expeditions to Hawaii and other adventures.

If you can still squeeze some divinity from the day, stop at **Jack London Village**, a civilized little shopping center that was originally a sawmill commissioned by General Vellejo in 1839. Wine Country Chocolates shamelessly and successfully dips just about anything in chocolate, and their confections are made on-site. The 25-year-old Sculpturesite Gallery recently has created installations all over the property with their works.

Distance from San Francisco to Sonoma: *45 miles*
Drive time: *1 hour*
Getting there: *US-101 N to CA-121 N*

1. FAIRMONT SONOMA MISSION INN & SPA: 100 Boyes Boulevard, Sonoma, CA 95476, +1 707.938.9000, www.fairmont.com/sonoma
   Details: *$329–$970 per night. Fitness and hiking classes included in price, as well as daily wine tasting 4:30–5:30pm.*

2. CAFE LA HAYE: 140 East Napa Street, Sonoma, CA 95476, +1 707.935.5994, www.cafelahaye.com

3. THE BIG 3: 100 Boyes Boulevard, Sonoma, CA 95476, +1 707.939.2410, www.fairmont.com/sonoma/dining/the-big-3/

4. SONOMA GOLF CLUB: 17700 Arnold Drive, Sonoma, CA 95476, +1 707.967.6272, www.castellodiamorosa.com

5. AETNA SPRINGS GOLF CLUB: 1600 Aetna Springs Road, Pope Valley, CA 94567, +1 707.967.6287, www.aetnasprings.com

6. LASALETTE RESTAURANT: 452 First Street East, Sonoma, CA 95476, +1 707.938.1927, www.lasaletterestaurant.com

7. THE FIG CAFÉ & WINEBAR: 13690 Arnold Drive, Glen Ellen, CA 95442, +1 707.938.2130, www.thefigcafe.com

8. JACK LONDON STATE HISTORIC PARK: 2400 London Ranch Road, Glen Ellen, CA 95442, +1 707.938.5216, www.jacklondonpark.com

9. JACK LONDON VILLAGE: 14301 Arnold Drive, Glen Ellen, CA 95442, www.sonomacounty.com/shopping/jack-london-village

What are you waiting for?

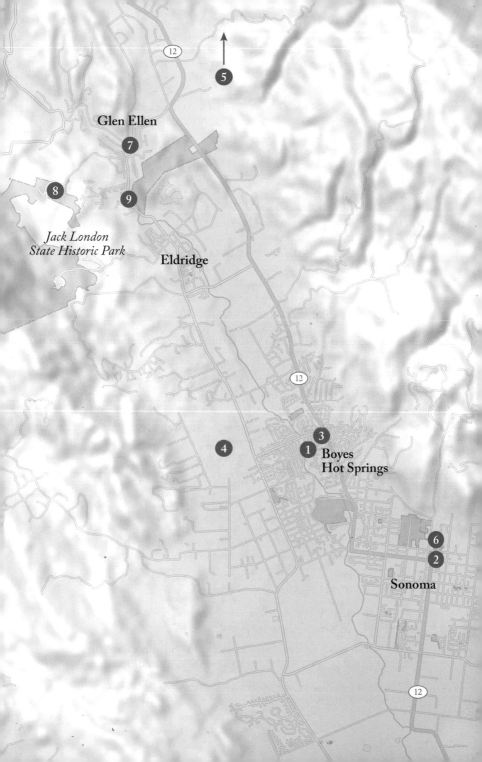

Wild Child · *Santa Rosa & Sonoma*

THE GIRAFFES ARE VISIBLE AS YOU STEP PAST THE ENTRANCEWAY OF **Safari West**, but when you saunter into their domain and perhaps get close enough for a doe-eyed encounter, close enough to see the buds on their rubbery black tongues, you can't help but feel the dense sensation of being completely absorbed in the present. While this is not strictly a "for kids" experience, if you are a parent, you are definitely patting yourself on the back during this spiritually awake moment. Sometimes you are on a family vacation that is really an adult vacation with playtime. And sometimes you just blow your kids' minds. Everything that follows is completely fun for grown-ups but most definitely a fantastic thrill ride for families.

Santa Rosa is the county seat of Sonoma and has many fine things to offer, but none so utterly unexpected as Safari West. On the north side of town, you will follow Mark West Springs Road (which is the locals' route to Calistoga and destinations east) and begin to curve into back-road terrain. The minute you get out of your car, the titillation of newness hits you with unfamiliar birdcalls, monkey yelps, and tires on gravel.

Safari West is a nature preserve that houses more than 90 species. The owners of the land, Nancy and Peter Lang, have been building their menagerie of mostly African animals since 1993, and their 400 acres are used primarily for education. Currently there are 900 mammals and birds on the property and you will see many of them. The organization is fervent about wildlife preservation and saving endangered species, and that zeal comes through the tour guides, many of whom have biology degrees and are there to further their own education as well as teach. Youth visits are part of Safari West's mandate to educate, making it a popular destination for school groups. This means that the tour guides are adept at sharing the safari experience in a way that engages your little adventurers.

The experience of Safari West centers on the tour. It begins with an hour of walking, so that you can take in the area nearest to the buildings and entrance, including the aviaries and monkey environments. You will see the flamingo meadow and watch cheetahs, fascinating in their restrained power, stalking the perimeters of their enclosure. After a break to get a snack at Safari West's convenience store or use the bathroom, it is time to mount up. Stretch your legs, because you will be

in a jeep for a few hours, though the time goes by quickly. (And yes, you can bring a beer along.) This jeep is a military auto that has been rigged to move with agility through the hills and outfitted with a rumble seat on the top, on which everyone can have a turn. Get a turn.

TIP: *The giraffes are on the early part of the driving tour, so try to take the first rumble-seat shift so that you can make eye contact with these gentle giants. Following the giraffes, you will ride by the rhinoceroses, which are also easier to observe from the top of the jeep. After that, you are on open road, scoping out animals that are easily seen from the lower seats.*

The giraffes are disarming and cute, like a hybrid of kitten and dinosaur with their geometric hides and long lashes, and since they are used to people, they will come within a foot or two of you. It is hard to look away from them, but you won't want to miss the other elegant savannah dwellers, like kudus, gazelles, and bongos, with whom they share a field. Southern white rhinoceroses are in their own area, so you are sure to see those, too. After that, you enter the main acreage of the property, where the animals are mostly left to roam wherever they choose. This means that you may not always be able to see them, but also that when you do, you get that shiver of discovery. You may spot zebras, wildebeest, the fiercely self-protective Cape buffalo, and Watusi cattle with their giant horns that would make a Texas cattleman blush.

If you are staying on the premises, you can head to the Savannah BBQ Grill to enjoy a hamburger or whatever offering is coming off the coals that day. If you are not an overnight guest, lunch is reservation only, so plan ahead, or stroll into Santa Rosa, perhaps, for a meal at **Franchettis' Wood Fire Kitchen**, a Sonoma County favorite with a casual vibe and simple Italian menu that is great for both kiddies and foodies.

The accommodations for guests on the preserve are technically tents but they feel very safari-luxe, with horned light fixtures, carved-wood beds, and views of the wildlife. The rooms can get chilly at night in Santa Rosa's African district, so close your window flaps and make use of space heaters. There is also a cottage with a kitchenette that houses four to six people, but it is not quite as smack in the middle of the wildlife experience.

Overnight guests are invited to roam the grounds at night without a guide. What do those sloths do when they wake up at dusk? And do the ring-tailed lemurs cuddle in their sleep?

TIP: *You will be treated to a symphony of birdcalls throughout the night, so if you are a light sleeper, earplugs will be provided upon request before bedtime.*

Day Two of your parental supremacy continues as you head east to the town of Sonoma. Not resting on your safari laurels, you're about to chug

ABOVE: *The stoic Southern White Rhinoceros*
BELOW: *The sociable flamingoes*

CLOCKWISE FROM TOP LEFT: *Pie of the day at Fremont Diner; Fremont Diner's front porch; pick a direction at Train Town; Train Town's pint-size fleet*

OPPOSITE: *Train Town has been delighting kids since 1968.*

into choo-choo central: **Train Town**, a theme park where the rails rule. But first, you'll likely have some hungry passengers by brunch time. Just outside of Sonoma's downtown area, among cascading vineyard-lined hills, is the **Fremont Diner**. A hipster haven with 1950s Southern-diner cuisine complete with counter service, fresh pie, and a chicken roaming through the yard, the menu is full of child-enticing options like ricotta pancakes and French toast, as well as hangtown fry and low-country shrimp and grits. The ambiance is old-fashioned friendly (lots of "What'll it be, hon?") and there are tables outside, so if your kids are still at a wiggly stage, you won't feel conspicuous. They are open from 8am to 9pm, the menu shifting from breakfast to lunch to dinner. From 3pm to 5pm, they serve only bar snacks. You can still wrestle a meal from the options but they are mostly smaller (though pimento cheese with toast and celery will keep you trucking till dinner).

Train Town almost needs no explaining. It is a town with pockets of amusements joined by train tracks. What is hard to appreciate until you are there is the scale of the place, which is built to a child's proportion. Even the tracks are delightfully tiny. The effect on kids is a sort of drunken excitement. All rides and other attractions cost money, but admission is free, so you can pick and choose, or just take in the mini village. In order to get to all of the offerings, you will have to hop on a train, as much of it is not accessible by foot. But why would you come to Train Town without some locomotion?

The tents near base camp at Safari West have a view of the giraffe pastures.

Distance from San Francisco to northeast Santa Rosa: *65 miles*
Drive time: *1 hour, 15 minutes*
Getting there: *US 101-N to Mark West Springs Rd*

1. SAFARI WEST: 3115 Porter Creek Road, Santa Rosa, CA 95404, +1 707.579.2551, www.safariwest.com
   Details: *Tents for singles and families available; $200 to $350 per night. Closed January and February.*

2. FRANCHETTIS' WOOD FIRE KITCHEN: 1229 North Dutton Avenue, Santa Rosa, CA 95401, +1 707.526.1229, www.franchettis.com

3. THE FREMONT DINER: 2698 Fremont Drive, Sonoma, CA 95476, +1 707.938.7370, www.thefremontdiner.com

4. TRAIN TOWN: 20264 Broadway, Sonoma, CA 95476, +1 707.938.3912, www.traintown.com

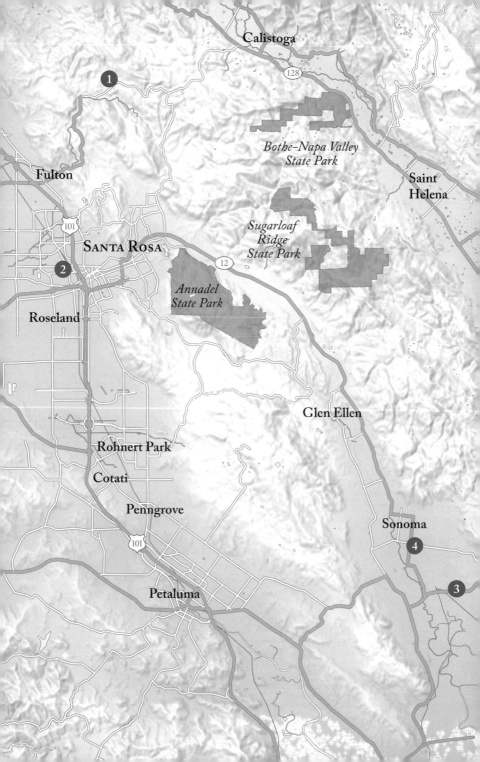

Freewheeling Afield · *Freestone & Valley Ford*

THE COASTAL SIDE OF SONOMA COUNTY OR WEST COUNTY, AS locals call it, has long been a playland for cyclists. World-class rider Levi Leipheimer hosts his King Ridge GranFondo race here for the same reasons that the back roads are full of be-spandexed enthusiasts weekend after weekend: gentle climbs, light traffic, gorgeous views, and temperate weather. Freestone is a stop on a very popular route and once you clip in and hit the road, you will understand why.

West County is dotted with cutely agricultural towns, and Valley Ford is one of these charmers. Start your route here by booking a room at the **Valley Ford Hotel**. Run by husband and wife Brandon and Shona, the small hotel in an 1864 farmhouse is also home to **Rocker Oysterfeller's**, a well-loved local bar and restaurant.

Across the street from the Valley Ford Hotel is the **Valley Ford Wool Mill**. Navigating west Sonoma County, you will surely notice lambs grazing the hillside. This area has been a sheep-ranching stronghold for over 100 years, though many families are opting to transition their coastal acreage to vineyards. For a long time, the cleaning and processing of the wool has been done out of state. To preserve the integrity of the fibershed, local artisans are now processing, producing, and educating visitors about wool. You can buy all kinds of custom bedding and other made-to-order products, or you can peruse the offerings on the shelf. Perhaps a wool blanket to strap on your backpack for a picnic...

Now you are free to blaze along the winding passages of the Marin and Sonoma counties borderlands. There are any number of gifts that come from a rigorous day of cycling, and a prominent one is the ability to ingest as many calories as you dare. There is no better spot to carbo-load than **Wild Flour Bread** (open Friday through Monday) in nearby Freestone. The 4.5-mile ride down Freestone Valley Ford Road is a primer for the pasture-lined hills you will roam through all day. The last mile is on Bodega Highway, which has fast traffic but a wide berth for the cyclist. Grab a loaf – goat cheese or the "Bohemian" (filled with flecks of apricot, orange, and candied ginger) – to have later for lunch and then indulge in a brick-oven baked Meyer-lemon-and-white-chocolate scone or a gooey cinnamon roll for breakfast. Take your coffee and baked goods into their open garden, which is bountiful nearly year-round.

TIP: *Wild Flour Bread is a cash-only establishment, so bring some bills — you will be really sad if you get that sticky bun in your hand and you can't take a bite.*

Home to 32 souls and a half-mile long, Freestone is a picturesque community and Sonoma County's first historic district. The town was anointed Freestone in 1853, so named after a public sandstone quarry. Originally a juncture in a now-defunct transportation network, it was a stop on the North Pacific Coast Railroad, which then connected to the Sausalito ferry. Salmon Creek, which defines the area's watershed, babbles through town.

Take in the old Western buildings still standing as you head down to **Freestone Artisan Cheese**, where you can pick up the rest of the makings of a beautiful picnic for the afternoon. The knowledgeable staff will slice into rounds for you, so don't be shy about sampling the mostly local offerings to find one that suits you and the loaf tucked under your arm. They also have beverages, cured meats, and pickles. There is a reach-in cooler containing a truly special item: Double 8 Dairy's buffalo gelato. The milk comes from a small herd of buffalo that live just down the road a few miles east of the Valley Ford Hotel and it produces the most pure and creamy-tasting gelato imaginable. The gelato is made right there at the dairy, in the true farmstead fashion.

TIP: *Take some gelato to go: the generous Freestone Artisan Cheese staff can often send you off with an ice pack to keep it frozen for a few hours.*

Once you're set for lunch and that cinnamon roll is kicking in, it is time to put some miles under you. The provided route (see opposite page), including the ride from Valley Ford to Freestone, is 19.4 miles. Depending on your level of fitness and cycling experience, you may find it challenging, especially if it's a gusty day, which can add a great deal of resistance. Elevations are as high as 1000 feet, though it's mostly rolling hills. The route is agrarian beauty the whole way, to distract you from any huffing and puffing, and well worth the effort.

When you cruise back into Valley Ford, you will likely be looking forward to a meal, a bath, and some solid rest. Luckily, you don't even have to leave the building to get all three. Rocker Oysterfeller's is not a generic hotel restaurant. It is an authentic local hangout, with food sourced from the fields you just tore through. Start off with a tapestry of their cooked oysters, including, eponymously, the "Rocker Oysterfeller," a play on oysters Rockerfeller, which consists of garlicky, creamy, bacon-rich mouthfuls. The rest of the menu has a Southern twang, and dishes like the buttermilk-fried chicken and oyster po'boy sing when made with pasture-raised birds and fresh-from-the-bay bivalves. And, hey, you earned it. If you aren't ready to tuck in after all that, the bar scene

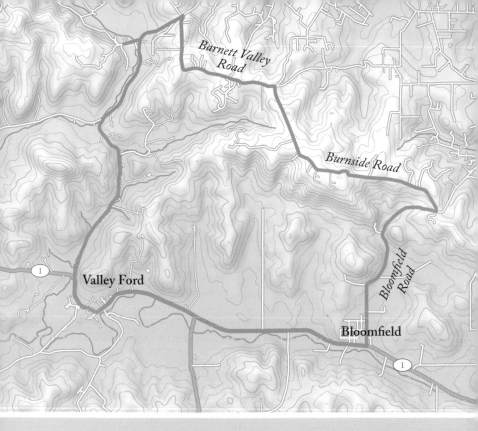

Head northwest on CA-1 N toward Valley Ford Estero Rd, .5 mi > Slight right on Freestone Valley Ford Rd, 2.6 mi > Right on Bodega Hwy, 1.3 mi > Left on Bohemian Hwy, .3 mi > Bakery break in Freestone! > Head east on Bohemian Hwy toward El Camino Bodega, .3 mi > Left on Bodega Hwy, .7 mi > Right on Barnett Valley Rd, 2.1 mi > Right on Burnside Rd, 3.3 mi > Right on Bloomfield Rd, 4.1 mi > Right on Valley Ford Rd, 4.2 mi

in the front room is a good place to have a brew and chat up one of the ranchers who make up much of the population.

The sun dawns on your recovery day. Rocker Oysterfeller's serves a hearty brunch to match its dinner, but if you want to move farther afield, you can take two or four wheels to tiny, verdant Occidental. Just follow the same route to Freestone and then continue on another four miles down Bohemian Highway. **Howard's Station Cafe** is a hopping breakfast joint offering a giant menu filled with old school health food options and a juice bar. You might have to wait for a table, but that will give you time to meander Occidental, a remote enclave that doesn't exactly want to be discovered, nestled cozily in the dank redwood-and-river landscape of West County. Like Wild Flour Bread, Howard's Station Cafe is cash only. There is an ATM in town, though, if you forget.

> TIP: *Check out the Patrick Amiot junk sculpture in front of Howard's. You can find Amiot's work scattered all over West County, especially Sebastopol's Florence Avenue, where nearly every yard has a piece.*

After brunch, retrace your pedal strokes to Freestone's **Osmosis Day Spa Sanctuary**. Osmosis has gifted masseurs and estheticians on staff, but their most unique and sumptuous offering is their cedar enzyme baths. Especially after a day of riding, the baths rejuvenate joints, muscles, skin, and moods.

Bathing in cedar is much better than it sounds. The finely ground cedar-and-rice-bran mixture is so enzymatically active that it gives off a steamy heat. After a tea ceremony and time to meditate in a private Japanese garden, you strip down and get buried up to the neck in this silty mixture. The bath is only twenty minutes, but if you get too warm, you can always lift an arm or leg out. Attendants come in periodically to pat your forehead with a cool cloth and lift a sippy cup of chilled water to your lips. Once you come out and get brushed down and showered off, you have free rein of the extensive gardens, which have an idiosyncratic mix of wildflowers and native flora and the geometric restraint of the Japanese style. You can even rent a hammock and take an afternoon siesta.

> TIP: *Book your bath and/or massage a few days ahead of time if you are coming on the weekend. If planning to do both, schedule the bath first, so your muscles are relaxed prior to the massage.*

Stroll across the street for coffee and biscotti in the Wild Flour Gardens (called Wild Flowers, naturally) before a leisurely ride back to the hotel. Turn off your phone and let the quiet seep into your bones for the rest of the weekend.

CLOCKWISE FROM TOP LEFT: *Sheep and goat milk cheese from Freestone Artisan Cheese; Wild Flowers garden supplies Wild Flour Bakery with fresh produce; the tea ceremony and cedar bath at Osmosis; Valley Ford Hotel and Rocker Oysterfeller offer small-town charm; Rocker Oysterfeller's ridiculously tasty oysters*

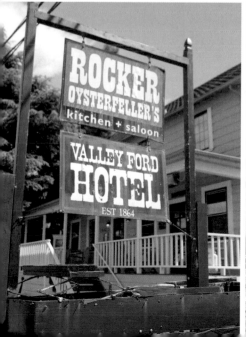

The intimate *Japanese garden at Osmosis is the backdrop to the tea ceremony.*

Distance from San Francisco to Valley Ford: *58 miles*
Drive time: *1 hour, 10 minutes*
Getting there: *US-101 N to West Railroad Ave to Roblar Rd to Valley Ford Rd*

1. VALLEY FORD HOTEL AND ROCKER OYSTERFELLER'S: 14415 Shoreline Highway, Valley Ford, CA 94972, +1 707.876.1983, www.vfordhotel.com, www.rockeroysterfellers.com
   Details: *Six rooms with private baths; $125 per night.*

2. VALLEY FORD MERCANTILE & WOOL MILL: 14390 Highway One, Petaluma, CA 94952, +1 707.876.1908, www.valleyfordwoolmill.com

3. WILD FLOUR BREAD: 140 Bohemian Highway, Freestone, CA 95472, +1 707.874.2938, www.wildflourbread.com,

4. FREESTONE ARTISAN CHEESE: 380 Bohemian Highway, Freestone, CA 95472, +1 707.874.1030, www.freestoneartisan.com

5. HOWARD'S STATION CAFE: 3611 Bohemian Highway, Occidental, CA 95465, +1 707.874.2838, www.howardstationcafe.com

6. OSMOSIS DAY SPA SANCTUARY: 209 Bohemian Highway, Freestone, CA 95472, +1 707.823.8231, www.osmosis.com

28

Chasing the Wind · *Bodega & Bodega Bay*

I KNOW WHAT YOU'RE THINKING, "KITES?! BUT I'M A GROWN-UP." Be prepared to leave that sentiment behind for a few sweet hours while you pick up the kite strings and feel your mastery of the sea breeze. And if you do have children, don't be surprised to find yourself negotiating with them for one more turn at the helm. Bodega possesses, among many other getaway bona fides, the quality of being the very best kiting destination. There are kite stores, long stretches of beach runway, and ample wind to get your kite aloft.

There are a few routes to the sea, but Highway One will get you on the vacation brainwave right away. Of course it takes a little longer, but you're navigating along the Pacific most of the way with hardly any traffic, rather than staring at the back of a bumper on 101.

> TIP: *There are plenty of scenic lookouts where you can pull over along the road to Bodega and take in the view. One of the loveliest is Millerton Point, 5 minutes north of Point Reyes Station on Highway One and just south of Tomales Bay Oyster Company. Park in the small unpaved parking lot and stretch your legs by following the short trail to the picturesque beach.*

Bodega has two epicenters. The first is the town of Bodega (population 220!), which is off the coast and home to various locations you will recognize from Hitchcock's *The Birds*, such as **St. Teresa of Avila**, built in 1859, the setting for the film's famous schoolhouse scene. That same year saw the "Bodega War," when Tyler Curtis, the landlord of what was then Rancho Bodega, tried to oust the farmer-tenants, who took up their hoes and shotguns and defeated him.

Five minutes past the turnoff to Bodega, Highway One curves right through Bodega Bay, which is nestled against the shoreline and dotted with seaside classics – chowder shacks, fine dining restaurants with views, saltwater taffy depots, and a wine shop that emails out the surf report every week. There is something innocently un-touristy and authentic about Bodega Bay. The town's scope remains small and the businesses are locally owned.

There are a few hotels and inns, but another way to go is to rent a house in **Bodega Harbour**, a serene community of beach-view homes

CLOCKWISE FROM TOP LEFT: *The Casino Bar and Grill; clam chowder is Bodega Bay's specialty; Candy & Kites saltwater taffy and colorful entrance; St. Teresa of Avila Church; crab pots outside the Tides Wharf*

that surrounds a golf course and has private beach access. Some are primary residences, but most are available as vacation rentals. Bodega Bay & Beyond has an excellent stable of options. If you are with a group of friends, you can stay in fairly luxurious digs with a kitchen, and often a hot tub, for much less than a hotel rate. You can also head to the fish market at **Tides Wharf** in Bodega Bay, pick up a bundle of fresh cod, oysters, and squid, and cook your own feast while watching the sun set from your deck.

Kiting gives you the most robust beach day. There is a bit of running around, chasing fallen kites or trying to find the current of the wind, and there is plenty of just appreciating the scenery and the sky. Once you get the knack for keeping the kite up for a while, you can begin to learn some tricks: loop-de-loops and dives or even a game of flying chicken, battling another kite for domination.

First off, of course, you will need a kite. If you don't have one somewhere in the garage, all is not lost! Head to **Candy & Kites**, just past the main concentration of Bodega Bay storefronts. It is hard to miss, with its impressive collection of unfurled nylon windsocks, kites, and flags flapping outside. In the front of the small shop is the candy department. Once you make it through the dozens of flavors of saltwater taffy, you will find the trove of kites in the back. Everything, from a simple diamond to stunning box kites, is available. Ask the staff for advice and pick one to be your airborne standard. If you want to learn kiting tricks, get a kite with two leads, so you can maneuver each side separately.

TIP: *Clam chowder is a local point of pride, made daily at almost every eatery in town. The Tides Wharf serves a fantastic and creamy classic version, if you need some sustenance on your way to the beach. And if you take your chowder seriously, go to www.visitbodegabayca.com to find the dates for the annual Chowder Day in January, where you can slurp your way through Bodega Bay and fill yourself to the gills.*

Once you have your new toy, you need only pick a playground, and Bodega is full of them. The stretch of beach accessed via the **Pinnacle Gulch Trail** from Bodega Harbour is perfect and less crowded than some of the other coastal spots (less chance of beaning a passing a dog with a falling kite). You can drive right up to the trailhead, even if you aren't staying at one of the homes there. The path down is gentle and easy to follow. Grab a partner to help throw the kite up and find your current. The hours slip by as you slowly become like the gull, moving inside the wind.

TIP: *One of Northern California's most challenging and beautiful public golf courses is the **Links at Bodega Harbour**. If you are a golfer, take a day to tackle these windy and stunning 18 holes. Greens fees range from $40 to $90.*

After running in sun and surf all afternoon, you will no doubt be famished. In the town of Bodega, there is an unassuming joint called the **Casino Bar & Grill**. Take a chance and step inside for dinner. The Casino is home to a pop-up restaurant that has been running for a few years. Thursday through Sunday, a roster of rotating chefs plans menus that change each night. One evening might be sushi rolls from bay-caught seafood and the next could be tacos and ceviche. They use local ingredients and keep the prices reasonable. This format allows chefs to play and experiment and the results are delightful.

If your love of kites becomes a habit, you will have a local fix to keep you going. In the Berkeley Waterfront Park (Spinnaker Way and Marina Boulevard, Berkeley, CA 94710), there is a kite park filled with amateurs and aficionados flying all kinds of airborne contraptions. Go on any day that there is a stiff breeze to join in the fun. In July, the park hosts the annual Berkeley Kite Fest, when hundreds of kiters come to watch and fly. You can see the spectacle from I-80 or join in the fun yourself.

View of the golf course and beach from the deck of a Bodega Harbour vacation rental.

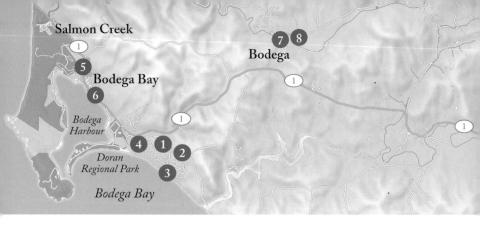

Distance from San Francisco to Bodega Bay: *70 miles*
Drive time: *2 hours*
Getting there: *US-101 N to CA-1 N*

1. BODEGA HARBOUR DEVELOPMENT (VACATION RENTALS): Harbour
   Way, Bodega, CA 94923
   Details: *Homes of all sizes available; most include all kitchenware,
   linens, and other vacation necessities; $130–$725 per person, per night.
   Visit www.sonomacoast.com for rentals.*

2. PINNACLE GULCH TRAIL
   Getting there: *From CA-1 N, take a left on Harbour Way to enter the
   Bodega Harbour development, turn left on Heron Drive and then left
   on Mockingbird Drive. About 600 feet on your right, you will find the
   trailhead for Pinnacle Gulch Trail, which will take you down to a quiet
   beach area.*

3. THE BEACH AT BODEGA HARBOUR: Access via the Pinnacle Gulf Trail

4. THE LINKS AT BODEGA HARBOUR: 21301 Heron Drive,
   Bodega Bay, CA 94923, +1 800.503.8158, +1 707.875.3538,
   www.bodegaharbourgolf.com

5. CANDY & KITES: 1415 Highway One, Bodega Bay, CA 94923,
   +1 707.875.3777, www.candyandkites.com,
   sales@candyandkites.com

6. TIDES WHARF: 800 Highway One, Bodega Bay, CA 94923,
   +1 707.875.2751, www.innatthetides.com

7. ST. TERESA OF AVILA CHURCH: 17242 Bodega Highway, Bodega,
   CA 94922

8. THE CASINO BAR & GRILL: 17000 Bodega Highway, Bodega, CA
   94922, +1 707.876.3185, Facebook: The Casino Bar and Grill

What are you waiting for?

Relaxed Riviera · *Guerneville*

THERE'S SOMETHING SO SWEETLY OLD-FASHIONED ABOUT SHOWING up in a town, parking your car, and knowing that your every vacation need will be just a flip-flop festooned walk away. Guerneville has been vacationville in this way for generations. It has had many iterations, from playland of the wealthy and powerful to the "Gay Riviera," and more recently, to a hip San Francisco weekend hideaway. Nowadays, it has the authenticity of all these eras in a well-designed package. Once you're off Highway 101 and the redwoods and roadside creeks take over the scenery, you are already on holiday.

Being that Guerneville has welcomed visitors for decades, there is no shortage of accommodations. If you are coming as a group or plan to be on the river for more than a few days, you might consider renting a house. For a weekend getaway, though, **Boon Hotel + Spa** is a delight. The rooms are sleek and modern. The pool has decadent recliners and a charming honor bar where you can open a bottle of local ale or pour a glass of Chardonnay for yourself and simply mark your name down. They also have a fleet of cruiser bikes available for all guests, which will easily sail you into town in just a few minutes. You may want to schedule a massage or facial at the spa for later in the afternoon, when you have had your fill of swimming, hiking, and sun.

TIP: *Don't plan on rushing out of the hotel too early in the morning, because breakfast in bed will be delivered to your room.*

Boon Hotel + Spa is just down the road from **Armstrong Woods**, which is a glorious way to lose a morning or an afternoon. This California State Reserve holds some remarkable redwood specimens, including the Colonel Armstrong Tree, which is estimated to be more than 1400 years old. The tranquility of these woods feels holy and the walk is gentle (although there are challenging hikes available as well – pick up a trail guide at the visitors center near the entrance). The duff of the forest floor is so soft in places that it practically calls for bare feet. If you want to have a picnic, there is a designated area three-quarters of a mile in, with grills available. On Main Street in town, you can stop at **Big Bottom Market** for artisanal deli treats or **Food For Humans** for more general provisions.

Tip: *If you are up for it, use Boon's bikes to locomote to Armstrong Woods during summer months. It is a flat and direct route, and while it is $8 to park your car, the entrance is free for pedestrians and cyclists.*

We still haven't gotten to the river yet! The Russian River meanders all over Sonoma County and there are many points of entry. Guerneville is the river town for a reason, though. It is a bit deeper and wider here, which makes for better swimming. It also gets just the right amount of sun. And if the temperature climbs too high, you can easily swim down to the bridge's shadow and take a break. **Johnson's Beach** has been a favorite for nearly 100 years and no Sonoma County summer is complete without a long, lazy float. It is not unusual to see a local gliding downstream with a beer and a smile. The parking is free but you can also easily walk from the hotel.

Tip: *Bring an umbrella or sun hat along with you, as there isn't much shade available on Johnson's Beach.*

Because of the beach's proximity to the town center, you can swim in the morning, towel off, grab lunch someplace, and then get right back into the water. There are lots of dining options on Main Street. **Boon Eat + Drink** (yes, under the same ownership as the hotel) has a fabulous Sonoma County wine list and sources their ingredients from the bounteous agriculture in the county. If you're looking to satisfy that post-swimming appetite, their burger will definitely do the trick.

If you aren't ready to plunge back into the river right away, there are several shops on the main drag to wander through. **Sonoma Nesting Company** is a particularly charming fine art and revamped furniture and knickknack menagerie, with a mind toward responsible re-use. The owner has a talent for merchandising and it is a pleasure just to see his tableaux of objets d'art.

Sometimes it is even nicer to be on the water than in the water, and **King's Sport & Tackle** will rent you a kayak or fishing gear for just such an adventure. There is absolutely no more beautiful view than that from a canoe or kayak in the middle of a river, especially this one. King's has

Johnson's Beach along the Russian River in Guerneville before the crowds arrive.

CLOCKWISE FROM TOP LEFT: *A guest room at the Boon Hotel; the hotel offers bicycles for exploring town; Armstrong Woods path through the grand giants; a display of items at Sonoma Nesting Co.* OPPOSITE: *Beet and goat cheese salad with toasted hazelnuts at Boon Eat & Drink.*

pick-up and delivery service, so you can take your kayak upstream as far as you like and then navigate to downtown, pull up to their dock on the beach, refuel with some grub and a beer, and when you're ready they will take you back to your car.

> TIP: *If you forget your inflatables, you can buy them in town or just rent them at King's, so you won't have to find a place for them in your garage when you get home.*

Nightlife in Guerneville has mellowed over the last decade but not to a whisper. A new tequila bar, **El Barrio**, is a chic option. There is also Dawn Ranch Lodge, which debuted in 1905 and opened their rebranded restaurant called **Agriculture Public House** about 100 years later. They have a beautiful bar and a fantastic outdoor eating area for a romantic evening. **Rainbow Cattle Company** is a Guerneville institution, as well as a gathering spot for the gay community, and has an event almost every night of the week (did somebody say karaoke?). You can also return to the hotel, grab a glass of rosé from the honor bar, and hop into the pool. The rooms have fireplaces, all set up to roar with the flick of a match.

Once you finally return to your car to leave town, you will have de-knotted, unwound, and rebounded the old-fashioned way, traipsing through timeless trees, listing down lazy waters, and letting your urges carry you from one easy hour to the next.

Big Bottom Market is an outlet for goodies, from chilled local wines to velvety chocolate sauce.

Distance from San Francisco to Guerneville: *75 miles*
Drive time: *1 hour, 30 minutes*
Getting there: *US-101 N to River Rd to Armstrong Woods Rd*

1. BOON HOTEL + SPA: 14711 Armstrong Woods Road, Guerneville, CA 95446, +1 707.869.2721, www.boonhotels.com, Details: *$140–$315 per night.*

2. ARMSTRONG WOODS STATE NATURAL RESERVE: 17000 Armstrong Woods Road, Guerneville, CA 95446, www.parks.ca.gov, +1 707.869.2015

3. BIG BOTTOM MARKET: 16228 Main Street, Guerneville, CA, 95446, +1 707.604.7295, www.bigbottommarket.com

4. FOOD FOR HUMANS: 16385 First Street, Guerneville, CA 95446, +1 707.869.3612

5. JOHNSON'S BEACH: At the south end of Church Street, just off Main Street, Guerneville, CA 95446, www.johnsonsbeach.com

6. BOON EAT + DRINK: 16248 Main Street, Guerneville, CA 95446, +1 707.869.0780, www.eatboon.com

7. SONOMA NESTING COMPANY: 16151 Main Street, Guerneville, CA 95446, +1 707.869.3434, www.sonomanesting.com

8. KING'S SPORT & TACKLE: 16258 Main Street, Guerneville, CA 95446, +1 707.869.2156, www.kingsrussianriver.com

9. EL BARRIO: 16230 Main Street, Guerneville, CA 95446, +1 707.604.7601, www.elbarriobar.com

10. AGRICULTURE PUBLIC HOUSE: 16467 River Road, Guerneville, CA 95446, +1 707.869.0656, www.dawnranch.com/agriculture-public-house

11. RAINBOW CATTLE COMPANY: 16220 Main Street, Guerneville, CA 95446, +1 707.869.0206, www.queersteer.com

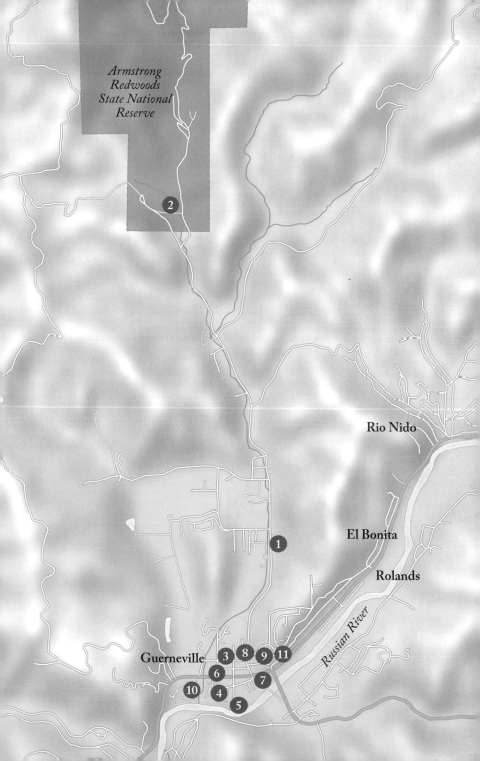

Armstrong
Redwoods
State National
Reserve

2

Rio Nido

El Bonita

Rolands

1

Russian River

Guerneville

3 **8** **9** **11**

6

7

10

4

5

30

The Fabulous Life of the Winemaker • *Healdsburg*

ROBERT MONDAVI, ONE OF THE MOST FAMOUS AMERICAN WINEMAKERS said, "Wine to me is passion. It's family and friends. It's warmth of heart and generosity of spirit. Wine is art. It's culture. It's the essence of civilization and the art of living." Perhaps this is what so many are seeking when they undergo the expensive, lengthy, and daunting task of opening a winery – an process far out of reach for most. But you can still experience some of the nicest elements of the winemaker's life without the Herculean effort – and in the span of one weekend – by simply going where the winemakers are and absorbing the lifestyle. Healdsburg, nestled in northern Sonoma County, is rich in this atmosphere, its aura centered around an old-fashioned town square, radiating out to residential neighborhoods and finally to miles and miles of vines. Here you can make the wine, walk the vineyards, and drink the essence of civilization.

Starting at the heart of the square, the accommodations are stylishly dominated by the Hotel Healdsburg group. Hotel Healdsburg is the grand dame and **h2** is the boutique-y little sister. The rooms at h2 are reserved in style, with lavishly deep tubs and luscious bedding. The pool is a scene for visitors and locals alike, with cocktail service and comfortable deck chairs. In the afternoons, they set out a generous culinary spread in the lobby for guests.

Winemaking requires a skilled palate, capable of understanding the subtlety of flavors at play in any given glass. Winemakers drink good wine and they also drink good coffee. There are many award-winning roasters in the county, but **Flying Goat** is not only a renowned maker of coffees, it is also a popular gathering spot in the mornings (and for afternoon pick-me-ups as well). Begin your day there with a single-origin drip coffee or a cappuccino, for example. While they also make great mochas and other beverages, the beans are the standout here, so let them shine. Would you add 7-Up to your Chardonnay? I think not.

> TIP: *Walking from h2 to the Goat, as it is often called, will take you through the square. If you take a right and trace the southern edge, along Matheson Street, you will pass* **Copperfield's Books.** *This small local chain has a solid selection of wine books. Grab a volume on area vineyards (or, heck, a novel, even) and continue on.*

Fueled and fired up for your day in the boots of a winemaker, you must next make a stop at **Fideaux**, the puppy boutique just a block from the square. It is imperative to have a dog to accompany you through the vines, and this is the place to outfit your little assistant with a handmade leather collar or find a luxe doggy bed. And, yes, you can also find a book on the winery dogs of the county.

Now it's time to get to work. **Bella Winery**, a Middle-Earth-meets-wine-country charmer with caves embedded in rolling hills, is a 20-minute drive out of town. The commute is part of the allure, as it takes you through a dense concentration of wineries, from big to boutique. Among the area's special landmarks are the white posts at country-road corners that point you toward every winery down each lane, a sort of alternative street-sign system.

TIP: *Just before you reach Bella, you will see **Preston Vineyards**. Stop in and taste how delicious organic wines can be. The grounds also include their farm, the fruits of which you can find at the Healdsburg Farmers Market on Saturdays from 9am to noon, going strong since 1978.*

Arriving at Bella, find your way to the 200-year-old olive grove, where you will be greeted with a glass of wine to start your Mixing It Up tour, which takes you through the winemaking process from vine to bottle, meeting the winemakers along the way. The old vine Zinfandel grapes are growing on-site right above the caves, and you will stroll through the vineyard. Winemaking is much about vigilance and observation, walking the rows, and tasting and tasting and tasting. You will try some of the current releases as well as the barrel samples (the wine before it is blended and/or bottled). The peak of the tour is the opportunity to make your own blend. After a lesson in picking out various flavor notes imparted by the terroir, you will work with three different barrel samples to find the perfect balance to suit your palate. If Joe Healy, the winemaker, is in, he will often stop by and pick his favorite of the group.

TIP: *This tour changes based on the season and even the day. During late summer, you may check the grapes on the vine for brix, or sugar content. In the fall, you might harvest some grapes and enjoy their heavy sweetness. Post-harvest, the focus will be far more on the barrel and bottling stage.*

The folks at Bella are also willing concierges to your weekend and can make suggestions for restaurants, tasting rooms, or even hikes you may seek, especially if you are looking to continue your oenological education. But after a long day of blending, it is time to unwind. Head back to h2, park the car, and enjoy the cloistered conviviality of the square, where everything you need is nestled in the center of town.

For an in-town tasting trip before dinner, right across the street from the Flying Goat is **Banshee**. Banshee wines are made locally but have an Old World appeal, with minerality and barnyard funk (that's a good thing). And the tasting room is simply a nice place to end your afternoon. The décor is a chic hodgepodge of found objects artfully merchandised, which you can purchase or just admire. There is also a record player that you are welcome to play DJ on from the house vinyl collection.

TIP: *Make an appointment for a Banshee tasting so you're assured a seat and the attention of their knowledgeable and warm staff. Though in winter almost all tasting rooms will be happy to see you, it can get downright slammed here, especially on the weekends.*

Now that you've tasted and mixed and meandered, it just might be time for a little something to eat. **Scopa** is one of several restaurants on the square and a favorite among wine folk. It is a long, slender space named for the Italian card game, which you are invited to play over dinner, with cards and rules available for the asking. The simple and

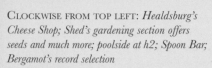

CLOCKWISE FROM TOP LEFT: *Healdsburg's Cheese Shop; Shed's gardening section offers seeds and much more; poolside at h2; Spoon Bar; Bergamot's record selection*
PAGE 213: *A rainbow arcs over the tasting room at Bella Winery.*

perfectly prepared Italian food is made from well-raised local produce and is an absolute joy with every mouthful. On Wednesday evenings, a winemaker is added to the serving staff – a requirement for being included on Scopa's wine list. It has become an endearing tradition, keeping wine stars humble and giving diners a sommelier with a story. The chef and owner, Ari Rosen, is especially brilliant with slow-cooked dishes like Tomasso's sugo Calabrese or porchetta.

TIP: *There is one outside table at Scopa that looks out on the square and seats four to six people. If it is a warm time of year, enjoy the long heat of a Healdsburg day and make a reservation requesting the table out front.*

A night out on the town requires a nightcap at **Bergamot Alley**, a quirky watering hole with a modular steampunk kitchen and other fixtures that give it the nickname the "Harry Potter Bar." Owner Kevin says that winemakers hang out there because "I don't serve their wines and they love that." His list is full of great finds and there's plenty of good beer, too.

After sleeping in a bit the next morning, maybe doing a few laps in the h2 pool, and detoxifying with the sparkling water available in taps on every floor of the hotel, you still have a whole lot of daylight to complete your winemaker's weekend. And as long as it isn't the harvest season, winemakers do take days off. And so shall you.

A short walk from your hotel is the **Cheese Shop**, a Healdsburg haunt for the most delicious and unique delicacies, starting, naturally, with cheese – wine's culinary soul mate – but extending to sweets (fig and walnut Italian caramels), domestic and imported oils, pastas, cured meats, ice creams, and any other rich treat your wine-steeped heart could desire. Doralice, the owner, is a wonderful guide, expert in her knowledge of every product, and a delightfully sarcastic cheesemonger to boot.

For some drool-inducing retail therapy, don't leave town without a visit to the **Shed**. This semi-ironically named glass palace of aspirational food, drink, and farming goods is a souvenir mecca. Organized by the categories of COOK, FARM, and EAT, the open-plan building has everything from hand-dyed Japanese Indigo tea towels to backyard beehive structures made from beautiful logs, to artisanal jams and heirloom beans. You can also tuck up at the banquette and nibble on some chicken-liver pâté and have a shim (a low-alcohol beverage), such as a pineapple guava with HomeFarm muscat and prosecco, or be like a winemaker and order a beer.

Wine is an expression of the earth and at its best is simple to enjoy, yet wonderfully complicated. The life of a winemaker parallels this – a straightforward connection to soil and sun, with an appreciation for the stunning nuances of life just within reach.

Fideaux in Healdsburg offers a colorful collar collection for high-fashion pups.

Distance from San Francisco to Healdsburg: *70 miles*
Drive time: *1 hour, 30 minutes*
Getting there: *US-101 N to Healdsburg Ave*

1. H2HOTEL: 219 Healdsburg Avenue, Healdsburg, CA 95448, www.h2hotel.com, +1 707.431.2202
   Details: *$250–$600 per night; includes breakfast and 3-hour bike rental. Pool, restaurant, and bar on-site.*

2. FLYING GOAT COFFEE: 324 Center Street, Healdsburg, CA 95448, +1 707.433.9081, www.flyinggoatcoffee.com

3. COPPERFIELD'S BOOKS: 104 Matheson Street, Healdsburg, CA 95448, +1 707.433.9270, www.copperfieldsbooks.com

4. FIDEAUX: 43 North Street, Healdsburg, CA 95448, +1 707.433.9935, www.fideaux.myshopify.com

5. BELLA VINEYARDS & WINE CAVES: 9711 West Dry Creek Road, Healdsburg, CA 95448, +1 707.473.9171, www.bellawinery.com

6. PRESTON FARM AND WINERY: 9282 West Dry Creek Road, Healdsburg, CA 95448, +1 707.433.3372, www.prestonvineyards.com

7. SHED: 25 North Street, Healdsburg, CA 95448, +1 707.431.7433, www.healdsburgshed.com

8. BANSHEE WINES: 325 Center Street, Healdsburg, CA 95448, +1 707.395.0915, www.bansheewines.com

9. SCOPA: 109A Plaza Street, Healdsburg, CA 95448, +1 707.433.5282, www.scopahealdsburg.com

10. BERGAMOT ALLEY: 328 Healdsburg Avenue, Healdsburg, CA 95448, +1 707.433.8720, www.bergamotalley.com

11. CHEESE SHOP OF HEALDSBURG: 423 Center Street, Healdsburg, CA 95448, +1 707.433.4998, www.sharpandnutty.com

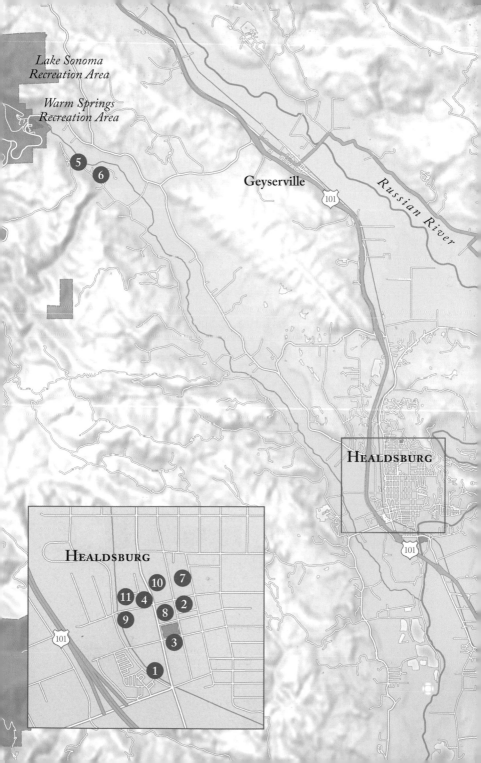

Lake Sonoma
Recreation Area

Warm Springs
Recreation Area

Geyserville

Russian River

101

HEALDSBURG

101

HEALDSBURG

Forager's Foray · *Jenner*

31

NATURE CAN BEGIN TO BE A TACTILE MUSEUM, AS WE WALK THE designated paths and allow the plaques to guide our movement and understanding. Foraging for food, for many of us, is an optional pastime, but for centuries it was one of the primary ways that humans interacted with their surroundings, not as observers but as a part of the whole evolving landscape. Learning to find edible plants gives a sense of belonging, curiosity, and respect. Mushrooms are often the gateway get, full of luscious umami. Since we haven't figured out how to commercially cultivate black trumpets, chanterelles, matsutakes, morels, or porcini, they can only be found. When your eyes tune in to the shades of the forest and you learn to spot the seemingly endless breeds of fungi, there is a palpable thrill of discovery. Of course, man can do a lot with mushrooms, but he cannot live on them alone. There are vast numbers of edible plants posing as nature, right underfoot. You need only know where and how to look.

Salt Point in Jenner is the only California State Park that allows mushroom hunting in the area. No Sonoma County parks permit foraging and though some national forests and parks do, they require that you obtain a free permit beforehand. Salt Point also happens to hold more than 6000 acres of deep woods with creeks and gulleys and beautiful camping spots, especially at the Gerstle Cove site, which has ocean views and is just a short trail walk from the beach. Gerstle Cove itself is the first protected underwater area in California. You can fish throughout the park but not in this marine reserve, which is full of subaquatic organisms to observe from land at low tide. Salt Point is competitive for mushrooming, so camping can give you an edge – wake with the sun and head out before cars start to fill up the lots and the pull-offs along the road.

> TIP: *Reservations are highly recommended for campsites, especially during high season, from April through September.*

Before you settle completely into camp on Friday night, stop in Jenner at **River's End**, owners of a very special sunset that hovers right over the place where the Russian River comes home to the Pacific Ocean. Have a glass of Sonoma County Pinot and install yourself on their porch until

CLOCKWISE FROM TOP LEFT: *Fort Ross;*
a foraging find and trail at Salt Point Park;
Paul Kozal's mushroom art
OPPOSITE: *The Russian River comes home*
to the Pacific in Jenner.

the color is drained from the sky. They also have cabin rooms that sit on the cliffs, if you prefer your foraging with a side of bed.

There is a level of knowledge that comes through experience, through walking the forest and finding a mushroom and looking it up over and over until you begin to know it. But before you even begin the undertaking of gathering hands-on know-how, you must educate yourself on the basics.

Foraging is a sacred skill, something passed from one person to the next. If you don't have a foraging friend, make one. Feral Kevin, or Kevin Feinstein, teaches the modern eater how to find all kinds of food in the natural world (www.feralkevin.com). He focuses his efforts on his own habitat in Contra Costa county, but you can engage his wisdom through his e-book, *Practically Wild*, a guide to locating and eating all kinds of wild plants, or by arranging a video chat so that he can help you ID your finds.

Educational opportunities abound in the Bay Area. The Mycological Society of San Francisco (www.mssf.org) holds classes and has an identification hotline for weeding out inedible, or worse, poisonous mushrooms after a hunt. In Gualala, you can also sign up for the opportunity to go out foraging with world-renowned mushroom expert David Arora (pictured on page 219), author of two of the most popular mushroom-hunting guidebooks in the world, *All That the Rain Promises and More: A Hip Pocket Field Guide and Mushrooms Demystified*, as well as photographer and gallery owner Paul Kozal. Paul creates stunning photo works from his mushroom treasures. These events are generally in October through December and end in a tasting of the gathered goods. Sign up in advance and then you will get word when the time is ripe (info@studio391.net). Forage SF leads forays in all kinds of wild edibles. After a day in the wet woods, a little butter and a sprinkling of salt is all you need to become one with the natural world.

TIP: *Many restaurants will trade meals for wild mushrooms. If you know of a place that has them on the menu and you are worried your own cooking won't do them justice, you might approach the chef and see if they are open to this.*

Waking to Sunday in Salt Point and closing up camp – with a wild onion and chanterelle omelet, perhaps – leaves you with a day to find your way home. Just north of Salt Point is **Fort Ross**, where the Russians settled in the early 1800s. The property has obvious merit as a lookout but was primarily used as a trading post for the quarry of hunters and trappers. You can take in the historical context by exploring the Russian-style buildings and orchards that remain from their settlement. And you might continue your foraging with fishing and diving for red abalone, during their season.

As you head back to civilization, stop in at **Café Aquatica**, which sits in the last oxbow of the Russian River. The worn-in-with-love wooden structure has a stage outside that often hosts musicians, and inside there are pastries and coffee to see you on your way. Forage a snack and return home, part of the whole ecosystem.

Built in the 1820s, the Fort Ross Chapel was the first Russian Orthodox church in the contiguous United States.

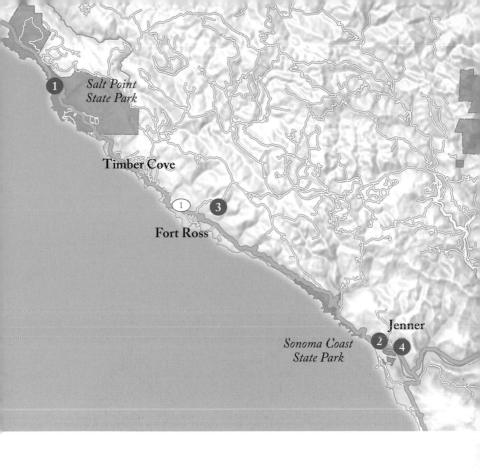

Distance from San Francisco to Salt Point State Park: *90 miles*
Drive time: *2 hours, 20 minutes*
Getting there: *US-101 N to CA-1 N*

1. SALT POINT CALIFORNIA STATE PARK: 25050 Highway One, Jenner, CA 95450, +1 800.444.7275, www.parks.ca.gov/?page_id=453
   Details: *Campsites $35 per night; group site $200 per night. Each campsite has a fire ring, picnic table, and food locker. There are restrooms and drinking water but no showers.*

2. RIVER'S END: 11048 Highway One, Jenner, CA 95450, +1 707.865.2484, www.ilovesunsets.com

3. FORT ROSS: 19005 Highway One, Jenner, CA 95450, +1 707.847.3437, www.fortross.org

4. CAFÉ AQUATICA: 10439 Highway One, Jenner, CA 95450, +1 707.865.2251, Facebook: Café Aquatica

32

Paradise on the Edge • *The Sea Ranch & Gualala*

THE SEA RANCH IS THE VERY LAST "TOWN" IN SONOMA COUNTY TO the north. Hugging a 10-mile strip of Highway One is a famous resort development that began a train of thought in architecture that is still relevant and admired. Once you cross the Gualala River, on its northern border, you are in Mendocino.

The Sea Ranch was purchased from a sheep rancher in the early 1960s and boasts the rocky pastures of Sonoma County but is also possessed by the wind-maddened beauty of Mendocino's coastline. The aim of the aesthetically unified constellation of homes and buildings is to engage you in this environment from every possible angle, to cradle you in the safety of shelter without ever letting you lose your place in the universe.

Though it isn't a gated community, the area is patrolled by private security guards, and if you are driving around or your car is parked without a pass, you will likely be approached by one. There are several coastal access signs off of Highway One where you can park and be on foot in the Sea Ranch, but to have unfettered access for exploring the enclave, you must rent a house or take a room at the **Sea Ranch Lodge** – which includes a hotel, a restaurant with imposing views, the post office, and a gift shop.

> *Tip: If you're just seeking a day trip, you can visit the architecturally in tune Sea Ranch Lodge, have a meal, and explore a slice of the coast from the trail that starts there and goes straight out to the cliffs overlooking the Pacific.*

You could naively stay in the Sea Ranch with no architectural knowledge whatsoever and still appreciate and delight in its intention. Because the idea is that no house blocks the view to the sea, that the windows allow you access to not only the ocean but to the marvelous meadow or remarkable rock formation outside, that the space inside is both open and full of distinct environments, that the roofs are slanted so as to allow the wind to blow right over where you are enjoying a cocktail at sunset. You don't need to read a book to understand this. Even if you never articulated these thoughts, you would know that you were entrenched in saturated beauty.

Tip: Weekend guests are welcome to use the recreation centers. The Moonraker Center is embedded in a small hill, making the pool a cozy enclave. The graphics in the men's dressing room are considered some of the earliest examples of "supergraphics."

You can develop a richer relationship with the place by downloading the free audio tour from the Sea Ranch Association's website onto your phone or listening device and using it as a cue to begin exploring the 60 miles of trails and understanding the history and philosophy behind the architectural choices. The tour was written and narrated by Donlyn Lyndon, one of the founding architects, who still lives in the Sea Ranch

Condominium One was the first unit built, in 1965, in the Sea Ranch community.

with his wife, Alice Wingwall, a talented artist. It is a delight to have his passion and experiential knowledge in your ear as you take it all in. The terrain is mostly coastal but there is also a more forested area of the development on the eastern side of Highway One that leads up through the hills to some expansive views at the peak. The homes can look quite simple until you learn just how detailed the mechanism driving their simplicity is. You will then understand why it is said by some that postmodernism, the iconic departure from skyscrapers and industrial optimism, was born here. (Download Lyndon's walking audio tour here: www.tsra.org/news.php?viewStory=1938.)

> Tip: *Many guests schedule visits to the Sea Ranch during peak mushroom-hunting windows because the forests and trails are known for their abundant yields.*

CLOCKWISE FROM TOP LEFT: *The eccentric Sea Ranch Chapel; Charles Moore's corner window in Condominium One; St. Orres hotel and restaurant; sunset at the Sea Ranch*

The Sea Ranch was designed to be a community of second homes and it still mostly is, though many residents initially bought their house as an investment, rented it to visitors for years, and then chose to retire here. There are several leasing companies that have vacation properties available and among the best is **Sea Ranch Escape**, which offers one particularly important property, Condominium One. Designed by Donlyn Lyndon, Charles Moore, William Turnbull, and Richard Whitaker, it was the first unit built in the development. In 1965, condominiums were a new concept; this early, architecturally significant example was placed in the National Register of Historic Places. Charles Moore's unit, Number 9, has been as he left it when he passed away, and his nephews are its keepers. Moore was an avid traveler and the spare design of the interior is wittily enlivened by his worldly treasures. This unit is an encapsulation of the Sea Ranch ethos, as there are views of the coastal crag and crash from nearly every room, including the coziest of benches along the western windows of the living room, a glass room that was originally an office but was turned into a bedroom once Moore was too ill to climb stairs, and the four-poster or "aedicule," as Moore called it. Four-posters are another common feature of the Sea Ranch homes. They are intimate loft spaces, often bedrooms, created on the second floor and supported by four columns. Unit Number 9 is not the only treasure by any means, and if you fall under the spell of the Sea Ranch, you can try out a different house each time you return until you find your personal favorite. For those interested in staying in the original dwellings, know that the development happened in stages, starting at the southern end and moving north.

TIP: *About halfway into the Sea Ranch is the* Sea Ranch Chapel, *built in 1985. Its own kind of architectural wonder, the nondenominational sacred gathering space is like a mystical creature that leaped from the nearby sea and settled in on dry land. Shells and urchins are embedded in the surfaces of the interior. The chapel welcomes visitors most every day of the year.*

Since you are renting a home, you will likely want to do at least some of your eating there. If you're with a group, part of the fun of the weekend is shopping and cooking for one another, sharing great wine, and divvying up dish duty. Most residents of the Sea Ranch do their "big shopping" in Santa Rosa, which is an almost two-hour drive away. Either stop there on your way or head to Gualala. The **Surf Market** is remarkably well stocked for such an out-of-the-way place. You can also cross the street to **Placewares** for some extra goodies. Placewares is a house of temptation for design fans, brimming with housewares and clothing ranging from Marimekko shirts to Chemex coffeepots to German dolls for little ones – all in a compact space that also hosts regular art shows. They have ceded a corner of their shop to the Market, a gourmet forager's handiwork. Fresh pasta, bean-to-bar chocolates, harissa, and other fabulous finds are there to up your dinner's ante.

> TIP: *If you aren't in the cooking frame of mind, head to Gualala's great architectural contribution, St. Orres, a truly unique and intricately designed hotel, with an excellent restaurant that specializes in using ingredients from the surrounding area.*

Come into Gualala on Saturday morning, stop at **Trinks Cafe**, get a well-made cup of coffee and one of their buttery scones, and tuck a Magic Bar in your bag for a hiking treat later. (Make it a rule of thumb to order anything that has the word magic in the title.) On Wednesday nights only, Trinks morphs into a dinner restaurant with a rotating menu that you can view ahead of time on their website. Do your shopping and then go back to the Sea Ranch and don't leave. You needn't leave. It's all there, just outside the window.

Distance from San Francisco to the Sea Ranch: *105 miles*
Drive time: *2 hours, 25 minutes*
Getting there: *US-101 N to W Railroad Ave to Roblar Rd to Valley Ford Rd to CA-1 N*

1. THE SEA RANCH LODGE: 60 Sea Walk Drive, The Sea Ranch, CA 95497, +1 707.785.2371, www.searanchlodge.com
Details: *$280–$450 per night. Some rooms are available for travelers with dogs (complete with doggie amenities and activity suggestions). January is the slowest and wettest month in the Sea Ranch.*

2. SEA RANCH ESCAPE RENTALS: 35590 Verdant View, The Sea Ranch, CA 95497, +1 888.SEA.RANCH or +1 707.785.2426, www.searanchescape.com
Details: *Homes of varying sizes available. Prices are wildly divergent, depending on rental dates, property, number of guests, etc.*

3. THE SEA RANCH CHAPEL: 975 Annapolis Road, Sea Ranch, CA 95497, +1 707.785.2444, www.thesearanchchapel.org

4. SURF MARKET: 39250 Highway One, Gualala, CA 95445, +1 707.884.4184, www.surfsuper.com

5. PLACEWARES: 39114 Ocean Drive, Gualala, CA 95445, +1 707.884.1184, www.placewares.com

6. TRINKS CAFE & BAKERY: 39140 Highway One, Gualala, CA 95445, +1 707.884.1713, www.trinkscafe.com

7. ST. ORRES: 36601 Highway One, Gualala CA 95445, +1 707.884.3335, www.saintorres.com

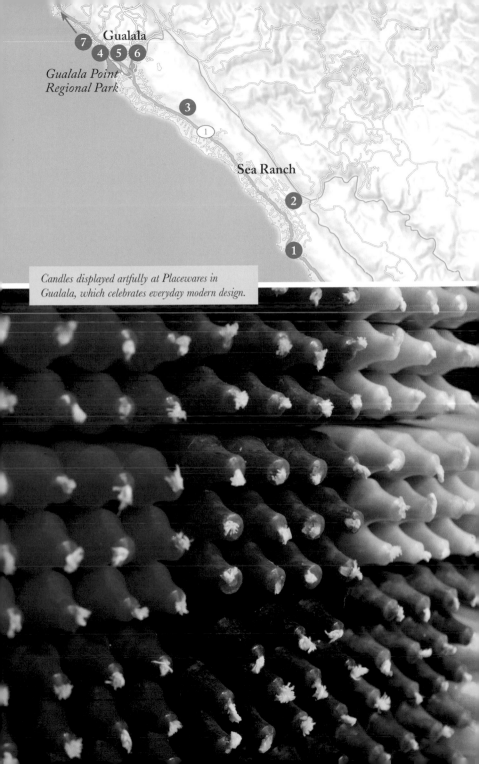

Gualala

7 **4** **5** **6**

*Gualala Point
Regional Park*

3

①

Sea Ranch

2

1

*Candles displayed artfully at Placewares in
Gualala, which celebrates everyday modern design.*

33

Gather Ye Organic Rosebuds • *Capay Valley*

RURAL AMERICA, AS MANY OF US IMAGINE IT, HAS BEEN LARGELY A myth for decades. Even in California, the fertile crescent of the United States and the source of most of the country's "specialty crops," almost all farming is really more aptly called agribusiness. Capay (pronounced KAY-pay) Valley exists in wholesome defiance to this trend. This area within Yolo County is still full of independently owned organic farms, growing an Edenic variety of fruits, vegetables, and nuts, and even practicing animal husbandry. Driving into the valley on State Route 16, which runs the midline, gives you an instant feeling of being cradled by the landscape, the scale of the surrounding hills and fields displaying the full breadth and width of the region.

Route 16 is the touchstone of a weekend in Capay, with small towns (small, small towns) dotting the road – between Madison to the south and Rumsey to the north – and farms stretching to the foot of the hills – Capay Hills to the east and the Coast Range to the west. You can experience rural life by driving up for one of the many harvest-centered festivals – celebrating everything from almonds and tomatoes to craft beers and gourd art – and take home some agrarian memories. Better yet, visit a few of the area's fantastic organic farms and take home a trunkful of edible bounty with those memories.

> TIP: *For a full calendar of festivals and fairs in Yolo County, check out www.visityolo.com.*

One of the best farm fests in the entire country is **Full Belly Farm**'s Hoes Down Harvest Festival in Guinda. Full Belly stands out as a real working farm, offering their more than 80 crops as direct sales to visitors, retail at farmers' markets, and wholesale; their farm stand is one of the valley's best (though only open on Friday afternoons). Held during the first weekend in October for more than 25 years, Hoes Down is a celebration of the harvest and a fundraiser for organizations that support sustainable agriculture. The festival engages all the senses, with workshops and seminars for the mind, great food and games for the body, and hayrides and singalongs for the soul. Even if you don't think yourself the bonding-over-a-campfire type, the conviviality of Hoes Down is infectious.

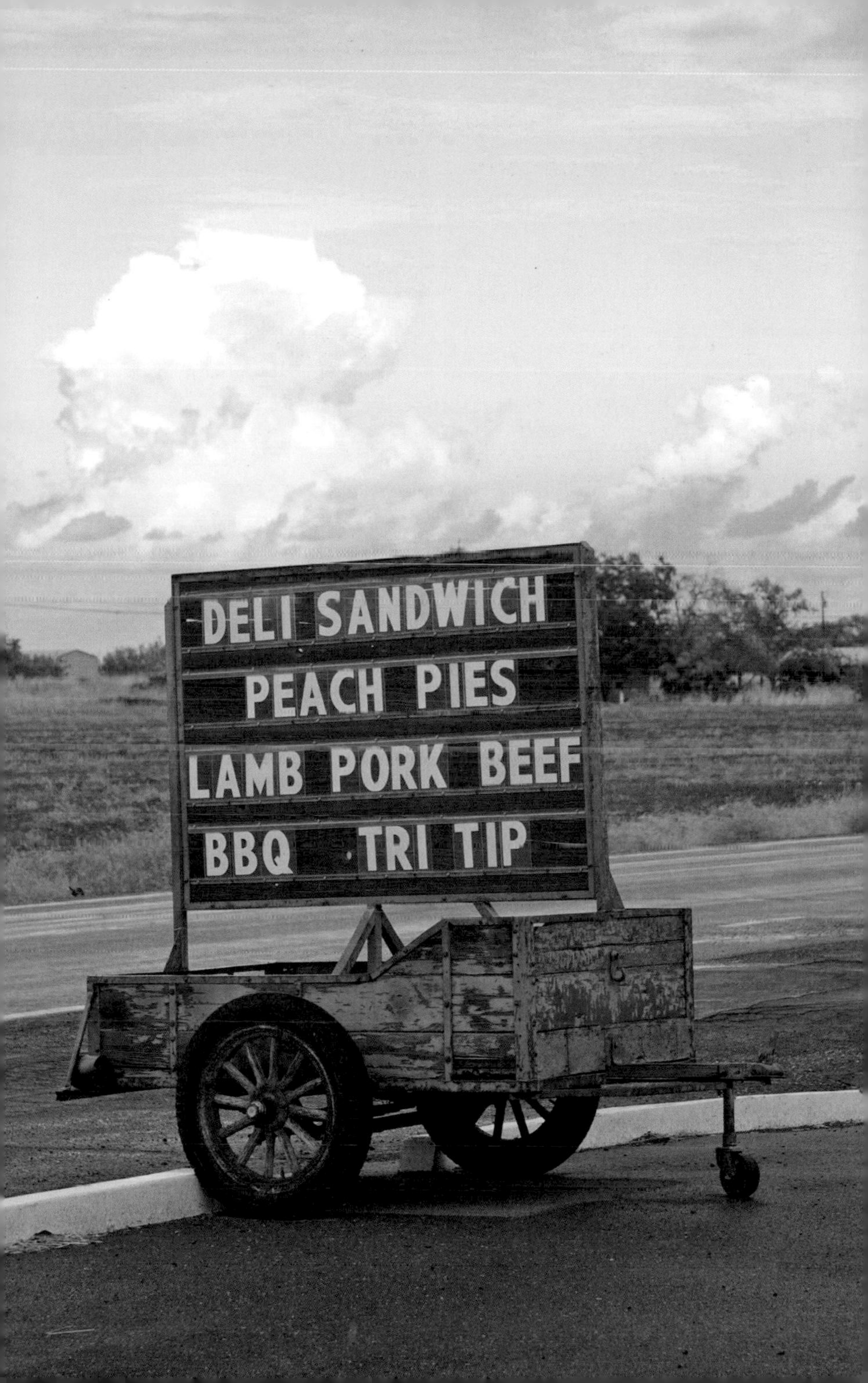
DELI SANDWICH
PEACH PIES
LAMB PORK BEEF
BBQ TRI TIP

CLOCKWISE FROM TOP LEFT: *Full Belly farmers-market flowers; Rumsey House; Guinda Commons BBQ; Riverdog's famous eggs; Manas Ranch offerings*

TIP: *If you like to camp or you forgot to arrange lodging in advance, the campsite at Hoes Down is a great way to extend the celebration at the farm: $25 per car and no reservations needed.*

If you are more of a mattress-and-walls kind of sleeper or are traveling to Capay outside of festival days, **Rumsey House** is a B & B along Route 16 in the town of Rumsey. The large home is craftsman through and through, with stained-glass fixtures and finely detailed woodwork. The innkeeper, Camilla Barry, travels frequently to Afghanistan and has filled the rooms with beautiful rugs and tapestries from her journeys. Breakfast internalizes the experience of your surroundings with ingredients from the nearby farms: fresh eggs, sausage, juice, and other hearty options to ready you for a day outdoors.

After fueling up at Rumsey House, head south on Route 16. Many of the farms along the road have stands, shops, or U-pick crops. Understanding how food grows and seeing it in the ground is not just a way to occupy a few daylight hours; it brings us closer to our humanity. As famed author and conservationist Wendell Berry said, "To cherish what remains of the Earth and to foster its renewal is our only legitimate hope of survival." We are not all going to spend our lives with our fingers in the soil, but we can make an effort to understand and support the work of those who do. And it's not too hard to appreciate this work – crisp, sweet apples; thick, juicy pork chops; and richly flavored tomatoes.

TIP: *For a floral foray, stop in at the **Cache Creek Lavender Farm** in Rumsey, open from 10am to 4pm, Tuesday through Saturday. They take lavender to all of its healing and fragrant ends, as oil, soaps, etc., and everything is made on the farm.*

Riverdog Farm is a must-stop in Guinda, but you'll need to call ahead to schedule a visit. While they don't have regular hours for the public, as a member of their CSA (Community Supported Agriculture), you receive their produce as a veggie box, which you can have delivered weekly if you live in the greater Bay Area. And they have world-famous eggs. There's even a *New Yorker* article by a journalist-cum-egg-zealot extolling the supremacy of the pasture-raised Riverdog hens above all others. Demand is so high that sales are limited to a dozen per customer.

After a few farm stops and before heading farther south, you may have kicked up an appetite. **Guinda Commons** specializes in Southern barbecue – East Tennessee barbecue, to be exact – where owner Richard Day-Reynolds learned the smoky ropes from a pit master named Charcoal, who always added two shots of rum to every recipe – for the tender of the coals, naturally. Wife and co-owner Lori Day-Reynolds covers the front of the house and offers up ten or so side dishes to go with the meats. "They change from minute to minute," Lori explains.

Highlights include white bean-and-bacon soup, a perfect vinegary slaw, and okra and tomato, each a rich and savory accompaniment. The grilled ham and cheese, with their house-smoked pork sirloin, is crave-inducing. Get the buttermilk-cream pie (or whatever pie is fresh that day) to go, if you don't have room after the savories.

The barbecue lunch should inspire any omnivore to pick up the finest local meats. Full Belly and Riverdog both sell meat, which you can order directly from them. For a retail experience, head farther south along Route 16 to **Manas Ranch Old Style Custom Meat Market**. A small meat plant in the back processes the Manas Ranch and other local ranches' livestock and they sell their own products up front. Beef, pork, and lamb are available in the form of fresh cuts and "further processed" products, like spicy Chorizo sausage or house-smoked bacon.

The most deeply embedded agricultural story in the valley is that of the Yocha Dehe Wintun Nation, a Native American tribe, which holds much of the acreage along Cache Creek and has been tending this land for thousands of years. **Séka Hills Olive Mill and Tasting Room** is the

modern interface of this grand history of stewardship with the public. There, you can taste the wine and oils grown and produced in the valley by the Nation. Tuluk'a – the Patwin word for "red" – is their blend of Syrah, Cabernet Sauvignon, Cabernet Franc, and Petit Verdot. You can also grab a decadent road snack at the deli window inside the expansive and crisp new facility, which looks out onto the mill floor. If you want to support the Yocha DeHe's endeavors in a flashier manner, cross the street and take a room at the **Cache Creek Casino Resort**, which has games of chance, as well as a deluxe spa experience (not to mention golf and acts like Frank Sinatra Jr.) for the asking. Take home a case each of wine and olive oil for the year.

The population and produce of the Capay Valley have changed as generation after generation has lived and worked here. What is as eternal as anything on Earth is that this land gives back to those who nurture it, and that spirit of nurturing has not been lost. To feed yourself with its bounty is something close to "our only legitimate hope of survival."

Walk the olive groves surrounding Séka Hills and then step into the tasting room to try the finished product.

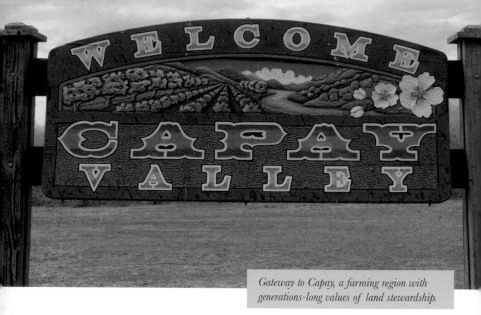

Gateway to Capay, a farming region with generations-long values of land stewardship.

Distance from San Francisco to Rumsey: *102 miles*
Drive time: *2 hours*
Getting there: *I–80 E to I–505 N to CA–16 W*

1. RUMSEY HOUSE: 996 Rumsey Canyon Road, Rumsey, CA 95679, +1 530.507.8811, www.rumseyhouse.com, camilla@rumseyhouse.com
Details: *Three air-conditioned guest rooms; $139–$149 per night. Includes breakfast, Wi–Fi, and hot tub for guests. Pets are allowed upon request.*

2. FULL BELLY FARM: 16090 County Road 43, Guinda, CA 95637, +1 530.796.2214, www.fullbellyfarm.com

3. CACHE CREEK LAVENDER FARM : 3430 Madrone Street, Rumsey, CA 95679, +1 530.796.2239, www.cachecreeklavender.com

4. RIVERDOG FARM: 7587 County Road 49, Guinda, CA 95637, +1 530.796.3802, www.riverdogfarm.com

5. GUINDA COMMONS: 7624 CA-16, Guinda, CA 95637, +1 530.796.0758, www.guindacommons.com

6. MANAS RANCH CUSTOM MEATS INC.: 26797 CA-16, Esparto, CA 95627, +1 530.787.1740, www.manasmeats.com

7. SÉKA HILLS TASTING ROOM & OLIVE MILL: 19326 County Road 78, Venice, CA 95606, +1 530.796.2810, www.sekahills.com

8. CACHE CREEK: 14455 CA-16, Brooks, CA 95606, +1 530.796.3118, www.cachecreek.com